ACADEMIA

Call For Papers 2019

Ties That Bind:
Love in Fantasy
and Science Fiction

Edited By
Francesca T Barbini

Academia
Lunare

LUNA PRESS
PUBLISHING

First published by Luna Press Publishing, Edinburgh, 2020

www.lunapresspublishing.com

ISBN-13: 978-1-913387-14-3

Academia Lunare CfP Series

Gender Identity and Sexuality in Fantasy and Science Fiction (2017)
Winner of the British Fantasy Society Award
2 Article Nominated for the British Science Fiction Award
1 Article Shortlisted for the British Science Fiction Award

The Evolution of African Fantasy and Science Fiction (2018)
Shortlisted for the British Fantasy Society Award
2 Article Nominated for the British Science Fiction Award

A Shadow Within: Evil in Fantasy and Science Fiction (2019)
[At the time of going to press]
Nominated for the British Science Fiction Award

Contents

Polyamory in Space: New Frontiers of Romantic Relationships in Science Fiction

Josephine Maria Yanasak-Leszczynski

Abstract

Modern Terran societies are built on binary relationships, from laws to television shows. While polyamory is on the rise, it will be a long time before we see its effects in our overarching cultural structures. Yet some science fiction works are already doing the work of imagining accepting polyamory as a normalized relationship structure.

When we look toward expansion into space, we see infinite possibilities. We find intersections between already formed alien societies, foreign biology and newly formed social structures to account for the random elements that will decide our fate in the great beyond. Books that explore the possibility of commonplace polyamory in humanity's futures have developed their approaches to it extremely differently. There is no standard lexicon when discussing polyamorous relationships in the future.

For instance, the protean gender and hyper-binary sexuality of Ursula K Le Guin's *The Left Hand of Darkness* clashes with the gendered maturation of the Grum and Aandrisk species in Chambers' *The Long Way to a Small, Angry Planet*, suggesting that when we imagine a binary set of genders fluidly, promiscuity is not always a requirement. In the *Dispossessed*, Le Guin suggests a principally nonmonogamous society that only becomes monogamous if both parties accept it and as long as both wished to remain so. Unlike so many current Earth societies, there is no expectation that monogamy is the norm or will be a state that lasts forever: "for better or for worse", as it were.

Robert Heinlein's *Stranger in a Strange Land* takes us back to earlier days of human exploration, when Mars and Earth were our primary planetary expansion. The polyamory here is imagined on a more personal, human level as we see Earth through the eyes of a Martian-raised earthling returning to the planet of his parentage for the first time.

Dune by Frank Herbert provides a more traditional view of polyamory, copying traditional models of polygamy toward the purpose of interplanetary empire. Published in the same era as Heinlein's work, it also shows that authors were both pushing traditional views of polyamory and inventing their own since early days of science fiction as a genre.

*

"History will call us wives." This is the final line of Frank Herbert's science fiction novel, *Dune*. It is advice given by the Lady Jessica to Chani, messiah Paul's long-time lover and soon-to-be concubine (1965, p.616). The world of *Dune* is a highly politicized space opera where family rules every aspect of one's life, and marriages solidify the place of both your family and self.

Chani and Lady Jessica occupy the role of romantic, but societally lesser, partners. Their role in the relationship is the pleasure and emotional support of their partner, while characters like Paul's later wife, the Princess Irulan, support their political interests and solidify their legacy. On Earth, concubinal systems of polygamy were not historically unheard of. In fact, polygamy with partners of equal standing also existed, but primarily in a heavily gendered and binary system with strictly defined roles and each partner defining half of a marriage.

Yet before *Dune* came out, science fiction was being published that challenged traditional views of relationships, and polyamory itself. Robert Heinlein's *Stranger in a Strange Land* (1961), introduces the idea of polyamory from the viewpoint of a Martian-raised earthling newly arrived on Earth. This work is often credited with launching a new era of how we think about relationships, and in turn changed how the genre imagined the future.

This paper will explore how works like *Stranger in a Strange Land*, *Dune* and Ursula K Le Guin's *The Dispossessed* (1974) explore the implications of publicly acceptable polyamory in human future spacefaring human societies. It will then compare those to the changes introduced when we play with gender and species in Chambers' *The Long Way to a Small, Angry Planet* (2014) and Le Guin's *The Left Hand of Darkness* (1976).

Polyamory is a rapidly expanding universe. In a paper Ve Ard (2005) cites that "a Google search on March 12, 2005 returning 177,000 hits simply on the word 'polyamory.' (Update: one year later, the same search yields 1,460,000 hits.)". They also express that "the concept behind polyamory, or the lifestyle of openly and honestly loving more than one person at a time, has been around for much longer than the word itself." (online)

With the exception of Mieville's *Embassytown* (2011), few works provide terminology, either invented for the sake of worldbuilding or our applied terms, to describe nonmonogamous situations. For the sake of clarity, this paper will apply standard terms proposed by Cheri L. Ve Ard and Franklin Veaux (2005). In this paper we explore romantic and family relationship situations that do not fall within the confines of monogamy.

For our purposes, monogamy is "a marriage in which two partners agree not to have sex or erotic love with anyone else." (Ve Ard and Veaux, 2005, p.2). In modern society on earth, this typically leads to procreation and raising children with primarily two parents. Many of these works reimagine this standard, or deal with remarriage in innovative ways outside of divorce and replacement of one half of the partnership with a new one.

A partner is someone romantically involved with another. In some works this refers to someone committed romantically and sexually to another individual, but it may also refer to the completion of a household, a mental/emotional bond or be quantified by a descriptor, as in the case of *sexual partner* (Ve Ard and Veaux, 2005, p.3)

Ve Ard and Veaux (2005) define *polyamory* as "the non-possessive, honest, responsible and ethical philosophy and practice of loving multiple people simultaneously." (p.5) This definition is often complicated by societal notions of ethics and what is considered "responsible" in a relationship. They go on to emphasize that *polyamory* means "consciously choosing how many partners one wishes to be involved with rather than accepting social norms which dictate loving only one person at a time." (p.5).

Even in invented societies, we see societal pressures to perform marriage or partnership in specific ways. Thus this paper's definition of polyamory will more closely relate to the second half of that base definition. Chambers deals with interspecies misunderstandings or prejudices against what may be considered by one group to be biologically essential to their understanding of relationships, while Herbert and Mieville provide rigid expectations with more or less socially accepted breaches of the standards they have applied in their worldbuilding.

Herbert's Duke Leto Atreides and Lady Jessica are the original monogamy transgressors: Jessica is thrown out of her ancient order for bearing a child to her royal lover, and the

Duke Leto keeps Jessica as a wife in all aspects except legal marriage. To keep him free and clear for political alliances, both partners agree that he may marry if it suits the interests of the House Atreides. This clearheaded and seemingly matter-of-fact approach to partnership is one of the many interesting interrelationship plot points of *Dune*. Yet it is not until she is forcibly removed from this partnership that Jessica invents for herself an identity worthy of the power she possesses.

In his afterword to the Ace paperback edition of *Dune*, Brian Herbert (2005) provides clarification into the mythical archetypes characters adhere to in that first entry of the universe. Myths and legends are regularly called upon to establish romantic norms and practices in human history. An attempt to understand not only forces we cannot contend with in the form of gods and monsters, but also a means to acknowledge and understand our own nature, many authors in science fiction have invented stories to establish standards within their invented cultures. For instance, Le Guin inserts semi-fictional interpretations of stories alongside official sounding reports in *The Left Hand of Darkness*, and Heinlein has Mike dive into tales like *Romeo and Juliet* in *Stranger in a Strange Land*.

These myths can provide a basis for marriage systems, but also define the roles of archetypes based on their interactions with each other. Herbert (2005) states: "*Dune* is a modern-day conglomeration of familiar myths.". The younger Herbert describes Paul Atreides as "the hero prince on a quest who weds the daughter of a 'king'." In this description, Irulan, keeper of the stories that frame *Dune*, is shrunk to the role of *king's daughter* (pp.681-682). What mythological role, then, do the Lady Jessica and Chani play in being the concubines of such heroic men?

Another house relying on its male head, much of Heinlein's

more novel entries to the worldbuilding of *Stranger in a Strange Land* (1961) can be dismissed as a male fantasy: three beautiful, young women live with and serve an aging employer who has all the gifts men wish they had. He's rich, he's capable, he's well-educated and talented. Yet with the addition of the foreign Man from Mars and a surprisingly flexible nurse, the household's already polyamorous communal set-up begins to spin in another direction. As the leadership shifts from the paternalist Jubal to the quickly evolving Mike, little changes in the male gaze of this little world within a now-retro future Heinlein has crafted.

Heinlein never escapes that male gaze; being a man that made much of his times, he is incapable of it. But he does paint a surprisingly complex picture of sexuality and human connection that elevates this sci-fi fantasy in between curtained group sex with various characters. After Jill and Mike have left Jubal's little commune, they become closer and interact on a more intimate level with various characters that flesh out a varied world.

Valentine Michael Smith (Mike) was born and raised by Martians after his parents died aboard their ship. His parentage is discussed at several points throughout the book, as Mike is heir to several fortunes, possible owner of Mars and other contested lineages due to the complex nature of his conception (Heinlein, 1961, pp.32-34). Aboard the ship, two heterosexual couples lived and worked closely, resulting in Mike, born from one woman who had an affair with another woman's husband. He was delivered by his mother's husband, who subsequently murdered his father after his mother died in childbirth (p.33).

This violent and mixed-up beginning is a foreshadowing to the fairly polyamorous and extremely open relationship Mike later takes part in. He meets Jill while recovering from his return to Earth. From the beginning of the book, much is made of his lack of exposure to human females. This sets the book up as a primarily heterosexual science fiction fantasy, though there are unexpected moments of queer elation.

Heinlein frames fears about Mike meeting his first woman in the conversations of his caretakers/imprisoners. These government and military officials discuss how painful it would be for him to see his first woman and then be forced to contend with not *having* her. While Mike is surprised when he first meets Jill, what they feared does not occur. Instead he is slowly introduced into the hyper sexualized household of Jubal Harshaw and when he finally loses his virginity, it is after a great deal of exploration and attempts at understanding how men and women relate to one another. However, in this turning point, the identity of the woman who first has sex with him is veiled, perhaps signalling that while Mike is always "in the moment" with the women he physically romances, he is in effect in a relationship with all of them (pp.362-364).

This is in direct contrast to the following chapters, which detail various interactions of Jill and Mike with people they begin having intimate relationships with as they travel throughout the United States on Earth. In particular, they carefully build relationships within communities they live in, then sleep with members of those communities.

There is some measure of strange force used in these interactions in the form of Mike's extraterrestial powers. Many of these instances and the sexual set-ups read like science fiction erotica, where women are levitated onto beds and clothes magicked away before the assumed sexual act (pp.388-392).

The framework for Mike's impassive relationship to commitment is somewhat based in his Martian childhood. It is repeatedly expressed throughout the narrations that he cannot process his surroundings like an Earthborn human and as he has never met another person, learns about them through whatever exposure he happens upon. Heinlein makes some presumptions about the nature of man and sexuality through his expression of Mike's maturation, but what would Mike's interactions with women be like had he not been brought to Jubal's poly sex cult?

Jill, an Earthborn human woman, is also changed by her time at Jubal's, and her exposure to this free and open household primes her for explorations into polyamory and what we might describe as swinging later in the book (Ve Ard and Veaux, 2005, p.5). Indeed, in the beginning of it, her relationship to Ben Caxton is tinged with his pressures to have premarital sex, which she rebukes (Heinlein, 1961, p.23).

Later, she described to Mike a change she has gone through and how she feels empowered by the nature of male attention (pp.415-418). There is some measure of male fantasy in these polyamorous displays. The women of Heinlein enjoy being looked at, they enjoy providing for men and they want to "give" themselves "all the time, to everybody." (p.412).

Jill and Mike's relationship begins with him, in his ignorance, being completely reliant on her. She has to dress and move him, telling him what to do and how to interact with his physical surroundings (p.77). There are already some overtones that can be read into Mike's usage of "water brother" as a familial greeting for adopted intimate partners, but Heinlein repeatedly tries to set this up as a more communal identification. Water brothers are family, but they are also good friends and allies. Mike repeatedly interacts with them in a sexual way, even eliciting Jubal, who he finds most beautiful of all, into kissing (p.7). Jubal firmly turns him down, but it is a curious inclusion in a book so preoccupied with the sexual and maternal uses of women. This concept of "water brothers" and group relationships spawned a very real group titling themselves after Heinlein's concepts and forming group marriages in the 1960s (Ve Ard, 2005). Morning Glory, one of the people involved in the creation of these group marriages, was the one to create the word "polyamory" as it is used today.

While providing new baselines for what it means to be romantically involved with someone and committed to their well-being, Heinlein was still chained to his own limited acceptance of gender parity and understanding of sexual relationships as primarily heterosexual, as well as between binary genders.

Empowerment is something rarely seen in the book, and yet it is an important part of polyamorous history. In this way, Heinlein may have been introducing explosive new concepts for the 1960s during a nascent Free Love movement, but it was not one that provided for the free choice and fully informed consent of participants. Mike himself is highly ignorant for the vast majority of the book, unable to speak English or think in Earthly human terms.

Jubal employs three women whose participation in the sexual practices of his domain is required as means of their employment. While it could be construed as sarcasm on Jubal's part, he at one point orders them all to kiss Mike as an "experiment" (Heinlein, 1961, pp.232-237). There are a few scenes where the power seems to shift from Jubal to the women, but at the end of the day, they are still his employees and men brought into his household expect sexual access to them (pp.358-359).

When describing the "bacchanalia, mate-swapping" of Jubal's "communal living", Murstein calls it "wholly moral" and credits its "patriarch" as "wise." (Murstein, 1974, p.522).

While interpretation of the communal, employee-employer system created in *Stranger in a Strange Land* may have changed throughout the years as lens shift from idealistic male ones into other minorities, it must be acknowledged that this invented work was an important landmark in Earth history and the genre itself.

Yet just like the free love movement of the 1960s, Jubal's commune is reliant on "'growing-closer' by [a] sexual union" that does not allow for the experimentation of genders amongst their like and the emancipation of the femme half of this slanted equation. The women are passed around in the name of sexual liberation and, while kissing is described very nicely, very little is provided to imply their physical and emotional needs are being attended to and their boundaries are repeatedly crossed.

Boundaries are a recurring theme in Ursula K LeGuin's *The Dispossessed*, which opens with our protagonist's entry into the "the only boundary wall on the world" of Anarres (Le Guin, 1974, p.2). As a world without marriage, words like "Bastard" have neither linguistic nor conceptual translations into Pravic (p.3). Couples may enter into mutual partnerships, but there are instances in the book of both open and closed partnerships, including the protagonist Shevek's parents. While young, his parents are separated by their work assignments, and he witnesses his father's loneliness with a child's distance. His father's sexual relationships seem to be discussed openly, but in cold, distant terminology like "copulation" (p.31).

Love and interpersonal connection are also recurring themes, but they do not require the exclusivity of monogamy to achieve them, therefore removing that boundary. Instead, Odonian society is based on a general concept of brotherhood and the shared experience of the collective as a baseline for interpersonal connection. Many of these concepts are presented in oppositions between Anarres and Urras.

The equality of the sexes on Anarres is regularly expressed not only in the general acceptance of women working alongside men, with generally accepted parity, but also in friendships which may or may not include sexual interactions. This being said, for reasons our narrator admits are inexplicable, boys at some point remain separate from girls. LeGuin attributes this to nascent sexual interest, attributing it to yet another assumption about sexuality and gender (p.41).

While there are several relationships that can be described as either open or polyamorous, the characters in *The Left Hand of Darkness* continue to be described by their gender, if not always defined by it. There are certainly homosexual and heterosexual relationships with multiple partners throughout the narrative, but the definitions of binary gender remain intact.

On the other hand, Becky Chambers (2014) experiments with gender fluidity without abandoning a binary understanding in *The Long Way to a Small, Angry Planet*. For instance, while readers do not find out much about Grum matings or family systems, we know that, like Heinlein's Martians, they change genders as they age. This is specified for what is more or less the protagonist, the human Rosemary, when she is introduced to Dr. Chef aboard the *Wayfarer*.

"I am a Grum, and I'm currently male," he explains (Chambers, 2014, p.38). Unlike Heinlein's Martians, Chambers' binary, gender-fluid species do not have caps to their abilities. While maturation is tied to gender, the female stage of Grum physiology is as active and strategic as the older males. We know that Dr. Chef had daughters, that he fought as a younger female, and that he is now one of the few Grums remaining. It is possible that the Grum employ a form of polyamory, as partnership is not covered in the book and is a recurring theme elsewhere. Similarly, polyamory, or at least some form of polysexuality, is possibly acted out by Martians on Heinlein's Mars, as the maturation differences between the genders make meaningful interaction between them seemingly impossible (Heinlein, 1961, p.392).

The attachment to binary gender expressions continues in Chambers' more experimental species, the Aandrisks. Aandrisk households are largely adopted settings where "egg parents" do not rear or care for their offspring. Instead, fully mature adults adopt the progeny of somewhat juvenile but fertile Aandrisks. These households may include groups of adults who enjoy sex together, or at the very least care deeply and are physically affectionate with one another.

Similar to Le Guin's "highly sexed" Gethenians, Aandrisks bond by attending hypercharged sexual orgies (Le Guin, 1994, p.96, pp.98-99; Chambers, 2014, p.302). Coming from this background, it is somewhat surprising that the more or less main character of *The Long Way to a Small, Angry Planet*, Rosemary, chooses her Aandrisk crewmate as a partner. During their conversations, both are careful to address the others' cultural needs and species based expectations, together defining their own standards of faithfulness to their relationship. For instance, Rosemary acknowledges Sissix's possible future desires to go to a *tet* and Sissix is careful to acknowledge human notions of standardized monogamy (Chambers, 2014, pp.298-302).

While a highly romantic scene, the blind passion that causes much of Terran based romance is replaced instead by frank discussion preceding a somewhat torrid secret affair. In this case, it is secret primarily because their arrangement is none of the rest of the crew's business rather than out of some perceived shame over the nature of their nontraditional pairing.

While a generally monogamous arrangement, the two share sensibilities about the necessity of their relationship's status as open. Or rather, both accept and welcome the sexual desires and required cultural bonding needed by one of the partners. This relationship and narrative in general are interesting because of the cross-pollination of cultural and species based arguments for relationship norms.

While humans have varied backgrounds ranging solar systems, monogamy is generally accepted cross-culturally. We see this not only in Rosemary's upbringing with two married parents, but also in Jenks' relationship with the ship itself. Not bogged down by notions of a body and sexual desire, AI Lovey repeatedly lets Jenks know he is welcome to have sex with human women (pp.60-61).

She acknowledges a physical need she does not require, and indeed Jenks often takes physical pleasure in her company, feeling the warmth of the mechanics of her core and touching the textures of her circuit boards and extensions of her fully realized self. Jenks refuses to have sex with other women, despite it being implied this might be a release for him.

Curiously, here too Chambers insists on keeping her non-traditional relationship model binary. Lovey uses she/her pronouns, and while arguing for the independence of AI, there is an argument to be made that Chambers has fully coded Lovey as a woman rather than simply a sentient.

Similar to other authors, Le Guin provides a radical version of gender fluidity but fails to escape it as a binary ideology. In this particular case, it's implied that homosexuality would also be an impossibility, as biologically Gethenians become either the inseminator or inseminated (Le Guin, 1969, p.96). Still, it is a queer sort of biological essentialism. LeGuin's gender fluid Gethenians remain binary, being described by her as "a race of people who are essentially sexless except for a few days a month, when they become very highly sexed either as male or female" (Le Guin, 1994, online).

The Ekumenical agent, Ai, is sent onto the planet Winter to see if they are "willing to communicate with the rest of mankind." (Le Guin, 1994) While there, he fails to avoid categorizing the Gethens into his own ideas of binary gender assignations. Le Guin discusses her own choices for the pronouns in the book's afterword as being the result of her having "believed then that the masculine pronoun in English was genuinely generic, including both male and female referents." She also admitted "This is a pleasant and convenient belief." (Le Guin, 1994)

Ai admits that he is "still far" from seeing Gethenians "through their own eyes." Instead, he sees them "first as a man, then as a woman." He highlights the baseline differences he sees as "categories so irrelevant to [Gethenian] nature, and so essential to [terran]." (Le Guin, 1974, p.12) Ai's own viewpoint backs up Le Guin's, or at least sets precedent for the rest of the novel, wherein all Gethenians are referred to as "he".

The first time describing Estraven, Ai describes him as a man, commenting in narration "*man* I must say, having said *he* and *his*." (p.5) While this may seem to delineate he/him/his pronouns and masculine assignation, Ai continues to refer to Gethenians as *he*, even when referencing their pasts as mothers, or current pregnant states. Additionally, motherhood does not create an identity for Gethenians for the rest of their lives, though Ai notes in turn that "no one is quite so thoroughly 'tied down' here as women elsewhere" by childbearing, and finally that, "[t]herefore, nobody is quite so free as a free male anywhere else." (p.100)

Le Guin also invents translational issues to cover the usage of he/him/his pronouns as inclusive of gender, commenting through narration that there is a word in Karhidish (one of the languages of Winter) which denotes a "human pronoun" (p.101).

Neither does their partnership create idealized two-halves-of-a-whole identities. While Estraven's partner, or at least their co-parent, provides for them after exile, the highly political nature of their situations makes them carefully separate emotional scenes we have come to expect from separated lovers.

This separation of sexual longing and partnership does not remove all standards of romance. After all, sexual tension between Ai and Estraven becomes a central theme later in *The Left Hand of Darkness*, and we see it as a central point of Gethenian myth making in the chapter "Estraven the Traitor", where two enemies enter kemmer together and ultimately bear a child (pp.134-135).

Here, in this particular geography of Winter, kemmering is understood as a "vow of faithfulness not to be broken, not to be replaced." (p.134). It is unclear whether this vow implies a monogamous promise or a long term connection between two people that would allow for different connections with others, but the ambiguity of Le Guin's sex-infused, close-curtained work allows for the possibility of either. Again, in another tale, a "kemmering by love and vow" is described as offering sacrifice for their partner (p.46). These vows are mentioned earlier as being "to all intents and purposes monogamous marriage." (p.98). This is not the norm. It is plainly stated that "Kemmer is not always played by pairs."

Le Guin's Ong Tot Oppong also claims there is no rape on Winter, yet there is a disturbing pseudo-religious scene that breaks with the cool, chaste sexuality of induced gendering (p.100). In a ceremony intended to provide answers from a future source, "celibates" take part in a highly sexualized ceremony where one of them is induced into what Le Guin accepts as physical feminine form by the repeated and clearly unwanted attentions of "the Pervert" (Le Guin, 1974, pp.66-70). This permanently physically masculine Gethenian's unwanted attentions toward their proffered partner brings the entire group into a frenzied vision sequence. During it, Ai interprets his surroundings in hypersexualized terms, referencing genitalia and his own sexual frustration, or perhaps that of "the Pervert", who must live in constant kemmer.

Ai compares the treatment of such individuals as comparable to that of "homosexuals" in "bisexual" societies (p.67). Here, as at several points throughout the book, Le Guin conflates gender and sexuality, providing *bisexual* as a means of describing a society that allows for two genders and requires they have sex with each other as proper course. In this same scene, Ai admits that "Karhiders discuss sexual matters freely", yet he avoids referring to the sequence he took part in as one reminiscent of group sex. This is despite the apparent aftercare provided to the kemmerer induced into the accepted feminine role (p.70).

The nature of kemmer as an overwhelming biological drive toward sex implies that partnerships would not denote exclusivity, unless they remained only in each other's company during their monthly phase. Genitalia, and later bodily changes toward easier pregnancies and child nursing, et cetera, are decided entirely by what form the next person in kemmer has begun to shift into. While the stories provided as literature and the later scene between Estraven and Ai provide exacting isolation and clearly defined binary sexual roles, not every pairing takes place in a hut in the freezing cold.

It is also implied at several points that politicians and the Mad King of Karhide have multiple partners. While they may bear their own children, they have also had their children born by other partners. It is noted at one point that "the mother of several children may be the father of several more" on Winter (p.97).

Mieville's *Embassytown* (2011) in turn complicates identity by providing dual personalities in single forms. This is similar to the infected Ohan in Chambers' *The Long Way to a Small, Angry Planet* (2014) but unlike that work, Mieville provides some insight into the romantic lives of these dual personalities.

Here we also have our first partnership that is purely emotional and involves completion of a household rather than a sexual component. The narration tells readers the protagonist and their "nonconjugal" husband try to interact sexually, but after failing still decide to commit to one another (Mieville, 2011, p.43). Both partners in this case pursue men sexually. It is also revealed that Avice was previously married to a woman.

Much like the complex worldbuilding of Le Guin's planetary dramas, the place where the characters live clearly affects their attitudes and options for partnership. While there are some areas in this universe that allow for marriage beyond the monogamous norm assumed by us here on Earth, the "homosex" Avice and her partner pursue is "a little bit illegal." (p.50). Here Mieville still accepts binary heterosexuality as standardized. Meanwhile, the political elite and alternative identities are exploring nonmonogamous arrangements and queer sexual practices that involve homosexual expression and possible nonbinary identities.

Avice is a more than coded queer character. She describes sexual and romantic pursuits with her husband, who references relationships with other women as well as a previous marriage to one (p.78). Her husband and her reflect on their sexual experiences together as a means of bonding, both sharing details and withholding different ones out of respect for their extramarital affairs (Mieville, 2011, pp.78, 87, 88).

In one recollection, Avice describes the sexuality of an Ambassador pair as "masturbation" while also refusing to fill her husband in on the explicit details (p.88). She alternatively expresses concern over his relationships, wanting him to stay safe from being caught in illegal activities. Here we see the basis of a loving relationship that is more than sexually open. While they have their disagreements, Avice and Scile share a strong bond they have built around the knowledge that others in their lives will hold their romantic regard.

Their marriage itself is at various points pointed out as a foreign concept. Yet the basis for households based on nonmonogamous pairings is firmly rooted in Mieville's far-flung societies: like Le Guin's *The Dispossessed*, Avice is raised by parents in a facility just for children. While it's mentioned that there children are sometimes raised by those who birthed them, societally at least some children are not being raised in a two parent household (p.16). They are instead receiving early exposure to households and child rearing as having multiple heads. These "shiftparents" care for the children as a job and a duty, similar to nurses in traditional Terran European houses or orphanage workers.

Avice's husband, Scile, comes from another planet where there are also multi parent households. While the question of them being polyamorous in nature is left ambiguous, during a quiet moment he posits the idea of children to Avice as a symptom of them settling down in her hometown. Here Avice reflects on her husband's ideas of a household, which includes up to six parents (p.82). Unlike Avice's generalized terminology for all of her caretakers as a child, referring to them as "mother" and "dad" before their names according to their genders, Scile differentiates what is assumed to be his birth parents, "mother and father", and peripheral, possibly non-blood relatives, described as "auntfathers or whatever."

Much like both Le Guin's *The Dispossessed* and *The Left Hand of Darkness*, Mieville's Avice is reared in a home by a group of adults devoted to raising children. Le Guin provided work for a third of the adults in Karhide on Winter in "the nurture and education of the children." (Le Guin, 1969, p.105). It is in this setting that Shevek learns his sexuality from the frustration of his peers, and a group education is also responsible for Mike's sexual revolution in *Stranger in a Strange Land* (Heinlein, 1961). Everyone is responsible for his learned behavior, and takes on the task of teaching him humanity's principles, including sexuality and a curious lack of romantic attachment in the traditional monogamous sense. In *The Left Hand of Darkness*, Le Guin tackles the effects of group education, as well as the differences binary gender fluidity in specific circumstances provides, mentioning on Gethen a child "has no psychosexual relationship to his father or mother." (1976, p.100).

All of these novels have some element of extraterrestrial spacefaring. Through these settings outside of the Earth and in exploration storylines, science fiction authors have been able to reimagine the basics of romantic interactions that have otherwise been defined as monogamous by humans for millennia. While many authors are still chained to notions of binary gender and homosexuality remains rare, these depictions widen the understanding of human interaction in fiction, especially when we imagine our future selves.

Additionally, polyamorous inclusions in these works are not limited to one-off examples. Instead, the presumption of polyamory provides a basis for worldbuilding. The effects of a multi-partner norm is seen from childhood to the family systems created in adulthood. Using the seemingly endless possibilities of outer space, these authors have posited polyamory as a future and a viable alternative to historical monogamy.

Ursula K. Le Guin proposed utopia/dystopia and alternative forms of governance that codified systems of polyamory as a peripheral future of humanity in *The Left Hand of Darkness* and *The Dispossessed*. Becky Chambers built separated societies of future humans whose interaction with and interest in other species created an evolution of monogamy that includes indigenous forms of polyamory in *The Long Way to a Small, Angry Planet*. China Mieville provides alternative understandings that are both legal and otherwise in the alt-universe setting of *Embassytown*.

Not all of these works depict equitable polyamorous systems. This is the case in Frank Herbert's *Dune*, which more closely resembles historical forms of polyamory in the form of concubinal systems. Gender parity is not completely achieved in these works either. After all, these systems are less an idealistic fantasy and more part of a real and viable world. Whether an evolution of humanity's attachment to monogamy generally, or a thesis on human romantic interaction, the worlds created by these authors would not be the same were they not to include the framework for polyamory as a basis for parts of their invented societies.

Bibliography

Chambers, B., 2014. *The Long Way to a Small, Angry Planet*. New York: HarperCollins.

Heinlein, R. A., 1961. *Stranger in a Strange Land*. New York: Penguin Random House.

Herbert, B., 2005. Afterword: *Dune*. Penguin Random House.

Herbert, F., 1965. *Dune*. New York: Penguin Random House.

Le Guin, U., 1994. *Afterword: THE GENDER OF pronouns*. Available at: <http://theliterarylink.com/afterword.html> [Accessed 28 October 2019].

---., 1974. *The Dispossessed*. New York: Harper Voyager.

---., 1976. Introduction. In: *The Left Hand of Darkness*. New York: Ace Books.

---., 1969. *The Left Hand of Darkness*. New York: Ace Books.

Mieville, C., 2011. *Embassytown*. London: Pan Macmillan.

Murstein, B. I., 1974. *Love, sex, and marriage through the ages*. New York: Springer Publishing Company, Inc.

Ve Ard, C.L., 2005. *Influence of the Science Fiction Writings of Robert A. Heinlein on Polyamory*. Available at: <http://www.polyamoryonline.org/articles/heinlein.html> [Accessed on 30 October 2019].

Ve Ard, C.L. and Veaux, F., 2005. *Polyamory 101.* [PDF] Available at: <https://www.morethantwo.com/poly101.pdf> [Accessed on 30 October 2019]

Finding the Female Quest in
Sarah Monette's *Melusine*

Cheryl Wollner

Abstract

In Sarah Monette's (AKA Katherine Addison's) fantasy series, *The Doctrine of Labyrinths*, she genders her male protagonist – Felix Harrowgate – as female. Though Felix is a cisgender man, Monette genders his character as female because he had been a sex worker, is raped, and is driven insane. Monette's characters go on a quest – similar to Tolkien-esque fantasy novels – but she diverts the quest narrative away from hero-saves-the-world. Instead of the traditional hero's journey, Monette writes a rape narrative and propels her novel by gendering Felix's experience as female. Monette's subversion of the quest narrative sends Felix on a female quest to find self-love. On this quest toward self-love he regains his sanity, and is able to possess language.

Felix is a male character drawing attention to the gendered attributes that seem to strictly divide a woman's story from a man's. This gender divide holds special prominence in speculative fiction, where man equals hero and woman equals victim or decoration. By isolating Felix from his masculinity and steeping his experience in the feminine, Monette requires readers to deconstruct the masculine-male, feminine-female binary.

In this essay, I analyze *Melusine*, the first novel in the series, through feminist and gender criticism. I draw on traditional fantasy sources, such as Tolkien's *The Silmarillion* and Joseph Campbell's hero's journey, to ground my analysis. I supplement this work with studies on female language and female authorship (*Madwoman in the Attic*; "Laugh of the Medusa"). I tie my analysis together with a study of rape narratives, female language and subjectivity within fantasy.

*

On Sarah Monette's LiveJournal blog she posted a list entitled: "Eleven things I will serve my best never to put in a fantasy novel unless I am trying to undermine them, and in fact could do without entirely from now on, thanks." (2006, online). Monette knew the tropes and clichés of the fantasy genre by the time she published *Melusine* (2005), the first book in her fantasy series *The Doctrine of Labyrinths*. *Melusine* follows the adventures of Felix Harrowgate – a former sex worker now wizard – and his half-brother Mildmay the Fox. Although her characters go on a quest – similar to Tolkien-esque fantasy novels – Monette writes a rape narrative and propels her novel by gendering Felix as female. Monette's subversion of the androcentric quest sends Felix on a female quest to discover self-love, regain his sanity and possess language.

Felix is a cisgender man, yet Monette genders his character as female because he was a sex worker, is raped, and is driven insane. The novel begins when Robert of Hermione – another member of the Wizard's Court – brings Felix's past as a sex worker to light (p.7). As Martha Nussbaum explains in her book *Sex and Social Justice*, sex work has the stigma of being attached to a woman's sexuality (1999, p.286). According to Nussbaum, moral society distains sex workers because "people committed to gender hierarchy" are "determined to ensure that the dangerous sexuality of women is controlled by men" (p.286). Due to this stigma, Felix struggles to admit his past and the powerlessness he experienced in the sex industry. He begins, "'I was a—'" but cannot say the word. He continues in narration, the only way he can come to terms with his shame. "'I thought for a moment I wasn't going to be able to say it, that the word [prostitute] was going to stick in my throat like a fishbone and choke me to death'" (Monette, 2005 p.8). Admitting his secret is akin to death, as Felix has built his life for the past thirteen years around a lie of noble birth and respectability. He holds respect only so long as his feminine past remains a secret.

As a wizard of the court, Felix holds the title *Lord* Felix Harrowgate, and gains power through this moniker. But the respectability of this position does not save Felix when Robert confronts him. Robert says, "'*I* wouldn't care to be seen with Felix Harrowgate'" (emphasis Monette's, p.6). He denies Felix his title and therefore his masculine identity as a nobleman. When Robert does address Felix as *lord*, he does so scathingly and positions it to contrast Felix's previous profession. He says, "'you haven't answered my question, Lord Felix. Do you deny you were a prostitute?'" (p.7) Felix's title is stripped of its power, leaving Felix in the passive feminine role instead of the active player in the conversation. As the novel progresses, the court officially revokes Felix's title. Felix then internalizes and distances himself from his masculine, powerful identity when he says, "'I'm not a lord.'" (pp.74, 91). He loses his position of male authority due to the female stigma of sex work.

Sex is also the inciting incident of the novel, when Felix's former master, Malkar, rapes him. As journalist Susan Brownmiller explains in the book *Against our Will; Men, Women and Rape*, "to simply learn about 'rape' is to take instruction in the power relationship between males and females […] *girls get raped*. Not boys" (emphasis Brownmiller's, Brownmiller cited in *Essential Feminist Reader*, Freedman, 2007, p.313). Being a survivor of sexual assault, Monette overemphasizes Felix's passive role as one who is acted upon. With each moment of the rape scene, Felix loses more and more power to the masculine character Malkar, who holds both subjectivity

and action. Malkar uses magic to lay a compulsion on Felix
to follow his orders (Monette, 2005, p.38). He gags Felix and
shackles him to the floor: "[Malkar...] forced first one arm
and then the other straight out, to where he could snap his
shackles closed around my wrists." (pp.39-40). Through the
verb "force" the language invokes sexual violence and keeps
Malkar as the actor of the scene. Although Felix establishes
that this act of sexual violence is commonplace in their abusive
relationship, (p.41) it *is* the first time where Felix is powerless
not just in the act of intercourse but beyond it as well. Malkar
channels Felix's magic in order to break the Virtu[1] and destroy
the Mirador (p.43). By the end of the scene, Felix loses his
magic, furthering his victim status.

Immediately after losing his magic, Felix recognizes he has
gone insane and states "Malkar has driven me mad" (p.45).
Later, Felix identifies further with his madness as a continuous
state of being, "I am mad, I tell myself" (p.207). Women and
madness have a history of being synonymous, and Felix's
madness stems directly from his female role as a rape survivor.
In the book *The Madness of Women: Myth and Experience*,
Jane M. Ussher (2011) understands the relationship between the
female and madness as one where: "women are at risk of being
mad, simply by being 'woman'" (p.65). Although Ussher's
book speaks primarily about madness as a fictitious disease
which women are diagnosed with for being either too feminine
or not feminine enough (p.65), Monette examines Felix's
madness as a legitimate mental concern derived from his female
role of subjugation. In his madness, Felix sees people with the
heads of animals and later cannot distinguish between his past

---

1. The Virtu is the magical orb that all wizards of the Mirador swear oaths
to. It holds protection charms to keep the magic of the Mirador's government
stable.

as a kept thief[2] and his present insanity (Monette, 2005, pp.44, 341). Furthermore, when Felix is mad, his narration reads in the present tense to contrast the rest of the novel, which is written in the past tense. At the opening of the novel, Felix's voice holds authority and he speaks with an educated vocabulary as he assesses his surroundings: "The Hall of Chimeras, having no windows, was lit by seven massive candelabra hanging above the mosaic floor like monstrous birds of prey" (p.5). But when Felix is mad, his flowing sentences are replaced with short, choppy language and a lack of understanding beyond his own body: "Light. I sit up. The darkness has been full of pain and screaming; I am shaking and I cannot hide it. Monsters booming at each other" (p.90). Monette raises the stakes of female madness by giving it a distinct voice.

Just as Monette plays into the trope of woman-as-mad, only to later subvert it, she also deviates from the quest narrative. Joseph Campbell (1949) summarizes the quest narrative within the hero's journey as:

A hero ventures forth from the world of the common day into a region of supernatural wonder: fabulous forces are there encountered and a decisive victory is won: the hero comes back from this mysterious adventure with the power to bestow boons on his fellow man (emphasis Campbell's, p.30).

But despite being the protagonist of the novel, Felix does not follow the hero's quest. Rather, Monette subverts the hero's quest in three ways: the call to adventure, the victory and the return.

According to Campbell, a herald of supernatural wonder

---

2. Kept thieves are children who work as pickpockets for adults known as their Keeper.

calls the hero to quest (p.53), and at first Felix's quest appears to follow this model. The herald's appearance seems mythic when Felix describes him as "a man, tall, redheaded, yellow-eyed, a Sunling out of a children's story" (Monette 2005, p.119). Yet, the man's coloring means nothing. Felix also has red hair and would have two yellow eyes, if one was not partially blind and therefore a clouded blue. As the novel progresses, this moment of the supernatural is actually ordinary. Each encounter with the man draws the narrative away from the standard call-to-quest formula. After multiple encounters with the man through Felix's dreams, the man tells Felix that he comes from the country of "*Troia* [...] *Where you can be healed*" (emphasis Monette's, p.287). Felix is not called to quest, so much as invited to be cured of his madness. Unlike Campbell, where "destiny has summoned the hero" who can then "go forth of his own volition to accomplish the adventure" (Campbell, 1949, p.58), Felix's adventure is not destined. It is a personal drive to find sanity rather than an adventure.

By the end of the novel, the Troians cure Felix of his madness and return him to his masculine state, yet Monette does not paint this conclusion as the victory of a mythic quest. Unlike Campbell's hero, who overcomes trials (Campbell, 1949, p.97), Felix's trials occur in the beginning and middle of the novel through his rape and struggles with his sanity, not through his physical journey. Throughout the quest, he retains his gendered passive role. Yes, Felix travels to Troia, but his half-brother Mildmay leads him there. Felix does not overcome his phobia of deep water on his own; Mildmay forces Felix onto the boat (Monette, 2005, p.348). And in Troia, Felix does not defeat his madness by passing a test or gathering supernatural aid, as Campbell's model suggests (Campbell, 1949, p.97). The Troians cure him, and though Felix experiences torturous pain, he wakes up and "felt well: peaceful, relaxed, cheerful" (Monette, 2005, p.393). Monette twists his narrative arc so Felix is victorious as the protagonist, but not as the hero on a mythic quest.

While Monette deviates from the call to quest and the victory of Campbell's analysis, she entirely avoids the return journey. *Melusine* is the first of a four book series and the novel ends with Felix sane, safe and halfway across the world from his home. Campbell's hero travels far as well, but his hero transcends the world of humanity then returns to the earthly realm to share enlightenment with others (Campbell, 1949, p.218). Felix and Mildmay do not talk of returning home until book two, well after Felix has achieved his quest. Monette deviates from the questing arc by leaving the arc unfinished, thus drawing attention to the framework of standard fantasy novels.

The heart of Monette's novel is not in the quest she disrupts however, but the rape narrative she crafts. Lynn Whitaker (2010) analyses rape in *The Silmarillion* where she reads a rape narrative underlying Tolkien's quest. Sexual violence as a central theme in fantasy novels places *Melusine* and *The Silmarillion* in conversation with each other. Monette is also particularly knowledgeable on Tolkien's writing. In her article (2005), "Doing Tolkien Wrong: Why Fantasy Shouldn't Follow in Tolkien's Footsteps", she argues that "Tolkien *chose* a quest-plot. He did this […] for a number of reasons. He wrote a great deal about traveling, so the quest came naturally to him" (Monette emphasis mine). The quest arc has become standard fare for fantasy writers but not for Monette.

Whitaker quotes Sarah Projansky[3] in order to define a rape

3. The definition comes from Projansky's book *Watching Rape: Film and Television in Postfeminist Culture* (2001).

narrative: "representations of rape, attempted rape, threats of rape, implied rape and [...] coercive sexuality" (Projansky cited in Whitaker, 2010, p.51). In Whitaker's article, "Corrupting Beauty: Rape Narrative in *The Silmarillion*," she examines how rape becomes a fear tactic and, more importantly, how it advances the plot (p.51). Aredhel's story is a rape narrative because she is raped by the Dark Elf Eol and has his child. The act of rape perpetuates a larger plot: Aredhel's purpose is to be mother to a traitor. She, like Felix, lacks subjectivity. And just like Tolkien, Monette uses rape to advance her novel. *Melusine*'s plot is simple: when Felix is raped and driven insane, he embarks on a quest to regain his sanity. There would be no quest if Felix was not raped. Monette engages in a rape narrative, gendering Felix not as the hero who acts, but as the woman who is acted upon.

Though Monette places Felix in this gendered state of madness, she does not perpetuate the rape narrative to be misogynistic. Monette's rape narrative follows more closely to the story of Luthien. Tolkien places Luthien in situations rife with threats of sexual violence (p.63-4), but in the end Luthien gains subjectivity. In the final confrontation with the villain, Morgoth, Luthien gains an active voice: "She was not daunted by [Morgoth's] eyes; and she named her own name" (Tolkien cited in Whitaker, 2010, p.65) thus imbuing her with the power of subject and language. In a contrast to Tolkien, Monette structures her novel in the first person so that Felix always has a voice even if he does not always have the words to understand or be understood. Through a rape narrative, Felix is given subjectivity in a woman's role.

Felix's insanity manifests in his inability to communicate with those around him. As *The Madwoman in the Attic* (Gilbert and Gubar, 2000) explores, femaleness is the inability to be understood. Though *The Madwoman in the Attic* speaks about female authorship, I will use a broader definition of authorship to include female speakers. As Gilbert and Gubar explain, women, both in reality and on the page, have been subject to illnesses including aphasia: loss of language (2000, p.58). In *Melusine*, when members of the Wizard's Court question Felix about the shattered Virtu, Felix hears the words but cannot process or understand their speech. He responds in narration only: "The words make no sense [...] I can't remember how to speak" (Monette, 2005, p.82). Even under threat of being burned at the stake for heresy, his answer is not spoken but narrated: "I can't answer" (p.83). His half-brother Mildmay later notices Felix's inability to speak as a recurring trait of Felix's madness. "[Felix] shook his head in a way [Mildmay had] learned to know and hate [...] it [...] meant Felix couldn't get to the answer, like the words weren't there for the thing he needed to say" (p.313). In his gendered role, Felix's madness prevents him from understanding and being understood.

Felix's gendered role culminates in Monette's exploration of a female language. Helene Cixous tackles the problem of women and communication in "Laugh of the Medusa" (1976). Cixous contrasts the taught masculine language to the feminine language that must be relearned, a concept that applies to Felix. For women, "[a]s soon as they begin to speak, at the same time as they're taught their name, they can be taught that their territory is black" (p.878). By Cixous' account, male dominated society does not understand the female language and purposely teaches women to abhor anything that brings their language forward (p.878). Being taught to speak properly is a key feature of Felix's story. Growing up as a sex worker in the slums, Malkar trained Felix out of his accent in order for him to pass as a nobleman. When Felix lies to his former lover that he is doing fine, he narrates, "I realized I had been about to say 'okay', that ubiquitous piece of Lower City idiom that Malkar had beaten out of me before I was fifteen. I did a quick panicky review of everything I'd said" (Monette, 2005, p.262). By being trained out of his native-born accent Felix learned masculine language – the language of the gentlemen of court. Because Felix's role is now feminine, he does not have the words to describe his female experience to himself or others.

But Felix cannot quest after the female language of Cixous because Felix is a cisgender man, no matter how Monette genders him in the novel. Instead, the language Felix gains provides a means to articulate his gendered position as a rape survivor. His language merges the language he has been taught to use with the language of his birth. Although Cixous does not provide a definition of female language I am comfortable attributing to Felix's experience, she does explain that "there is no general woman, no one typical woman" (Cixous, 1976 p.876). Felix's gendered role is no less valid at giving voice to the feminine. Writing or speaking with one's body does not only belong to cisgender women. By the end of the novel, Felix speaks confidently about his hitherto assigned female role. The people of Troia misunderstand Felix and Mildmay's situation and believe Mildmay caused Felix's madness due to sustained physical abuse. The Troian who heals Felix questions Felix's devotion to Mildmay and asks, "'Do you think a common hired murderer deserves this kind of loyalty?'" Felix responds: "'Why not, from a prostitute?'" (Monette, 2005, p.411). This is the first time Felix openly admits to his past and it is all the more powerful because no one presses him to do so. The negative connotation of sex work as a woman's profession is gone. Felix has come to a place of self-acceptance where femaleness is no longer shameful.

Felix continues to release himself from the self-abhorrence of femaleness when he tells Mildmay that Malkar raped him.

> 'Malkar broke the Virtu by means of a spell that he cast on me […] and the way that he worked the spell was…' I couldn't say it. I couldn't get the words out […] 'He raped me […] *He raped me*. He raped me and used me to break the Virtu and drove me mad' (Monette, 2005, p.418 emphasis Monette's).

Not only does Felix gain access to language through his quest, but he also removes the gendered taboo from his experience. He takes ownership of his past and attributes the action of rape to Malkar. In a final reclamation of speech, Felix tells Mildmay: "'It's okay,' I said, using the word deliberately" (p. 418). Felix has moved beyond his taught male language, which could not encompass his female experience or understand the language of his birth.

Without his madness, Monette no longer genders Felix female, yet his female experience remains valid. Monette structures her novel around his gendered role to give the feminine a voice and then show that this voice does not solely belong to women. Felix resembles the woman of the rape narrative far more than he does the hero of the quest narrative, yet he inhabits both roles simultaneously. He is a male character drawing attention to the gendered attributes that seem to strictly divide a woman's story from a man's. This gender divide is especially prominent in speculative fiction, where men are heroes and women are victims or decoration. By isolating Felix from his masculinity and steeping his experience in the feminine, Monette requires readers to deconstruct the masculine-male, feminine-female binary. As *The Doctrine of Labyrinths* series is speculative fiction, Monette decides what in her world will be the same or different from our world. She decides what is valued (masculinity, femininity, both, neither), as well as how her fantasy world accepts (or rejects) the gender binary. Her critique of androcentric narratives that deny women agency extends beyond Felix's characterization. She subverts the quest narrative and though Felix does not discover a female language, he embarks on a female quest and learns self-love over self-abhorrence.

Bibliography

Campbell, J., 1949. *The Hero with a Thousand Faces*. New York: Pantheon Books.

Cixous, H., 1976. Laugh of the Medusa. *The University of Chicago Press*, 1(4), pp.875-893.

Freedman, E.B. ed., 2007. *The Essential Feminist Reader.* New York: The Modern Library.

Gilbert, S.M. and Gubar, S., 2000. Infection in the Sentence: The Woman Writer and the Anxiety of Authorship. *The Madwoman in the Attic: The Woman Writer and the Nineteenth-Century Literary Imagination*. 2nd Edition. New Haven, CT: Yale New Haven Press, pp.45-92.

Monette, S., 2005. *Melusine*. New York: Penguin Group.

---., 2005b. Doing Tolkien Wrong: Why Fantasy Shouldn't Follow in Tolkien's Footsteps. *Reflection's Edge*. (e-zine permanently closed).

---., 2006. Eleven things I will serve my best never to put in a fantasy novel unless I am trying to undermine them, and in fact could do without entirely from now on, thanks. *LiveJournal.* Available at: *<truepenny.livejournal. com>* [Accessed on 29 February 2020].

Nussbaum, M. C., 1999. Whether for Reason or Prejudice' Taking Money for Bodily Services. *Sex and Social Justice*. Oxford: Oxford University Press, pp.276-298.

Ussher, J., 2011. Labeling Women as Mad: Regulating and Oppressing Women. *The Madness of Women: Myth and Experience*. New York: Psychology Press, pp.64-110.

Whitaker, L., 2010. Corrupting Beauty: Rape Narrative in *The Silmarillion. Mythlore: A Journal of J.R.R. Tokien, C.S. Lewis, Charles Williams, and Mythopoeic Literature* 29 (2010 Fall-Winter), pp.51-68.

Robot Love is Queer

Cheryl Morgan

Abstract

In an interview for *The Guardian*, Ian McEwan suggested that his latest novel, *Machines Like Me*, would be innovative in treating the issue of relationships between humans and robots, because most science fiction is about "travelling at 10 times the speed of light in anti-gravity boots". While McEwan has since been at pains to point out that he doesn't hate science fiction, and has even read some of it, his knowledge of the genre still seems lacking. Romantic liaisons between humans and artificial beings can be traced back at least as far as the ancient Greek story of the Pandora, who was created by the Smith God Hēphaistos specifically to seduce mortal men.

There is so much robot love in the history of science fiction that any attempt to examine it in a mere essay would end up more like a catalogue of stories. For this essay, therefore, I propose to concentrate on how science fiction writers use human-robot relations as a means of talking about forbidden love, and in particular diverse sexualities. Loving a robot is loving The Other.

The title of the essay is a quote from Janelle Monáe's album, *Electric Lady*. The future history tale that Monáe tells in *Metropolis*, *The Archandroid* and *Electric Lady* is centred on the illegal love affair between the android rights activist, Cindi Mayweather, and her human beau, Anthony Greendown.

Other works I will be mentioning will include the Imperial Radch Trilogy by Anne Leckie, *Autonomous* by Analee Newitz and *Rosewater Insurrection* by Tade Thompson.

*

"It is true we shall be monsters, cut off from the world; but on that account we shall be more attached to one another. Our lives will not be happy, but they will be harmless, and free from the misery I now feel." – Mary Shelley, *Frankenstein*

In an interview for *The Guardian*, Ian McEwan suggested that his latest novel, *Machines Like Me*, would be innovative in treating the issue of relationships between humans and robots, because most science fiction is about "travelling at 10 times the speed of light in anti-gravity boots" (Adams, 2019). While McEwan has since been at pains to point out that he doesn't hate science fiction, and has even read some of it (Bourgois, 2019), his knowledge of the genre still seems lacking. Romantic liaisons between humans and artificial beings have a long and honourable tradition in speculative fiction. A much more interesting story waits to be told.

A prime candidate for the title of the first sexbot in literature is the being known as Pandora. We tend to think of her as a mortal girl, but close reading of the myth suggests otherwise. Pandora was created to seduce Epimetheus, the foolish brother of Prometheus. Zeus knew that, once installed in the brothers' household, she could be relied upon to innocently unleash his box of horrors on mankind in revenge for Prometheus having given us the gift of fire. But Zeus did not make Pandora himself. Instead he delegated the job to the smith god Hēphaistos, and when Hēphaistos made something he generally made it from metal.

We know that Hēphaistos made artificial beings. Homer tells us that his forge was staffed by a bevy of beautiful golden maidens – Kourai Khryseai – whom the god had made to act as his servants. He also made several metal monsters, such as the fire-breathing bulls that he gifted to King Aeetes of Colchis. It seems entirely reasonable that he would have made the lovely

Pandora from metal as well (Mayor, 2018).

The honour of being the first sexbot in modern literature probably falls to Olympia, a character from ETA (Ernst) Hoffmann's self-starring story suite known as *The Tales of Hoffmann*. A 19th Century German writer of Gothic horror, Hoffmann's works have been used as the basis for a number

of operas, including Tchaikovsky's *The Nutcracker*. The Tales is a collection of three short stories describing fantastical adventures. In the first of these, titled "The Sandman", a young man called Nathanael falls in love with Olympia, a singing automaton created by a scientist called Spalanzani and the spectacle-maker, Dr Coppelius (Hoffmann, 1815). It is a pair of magical glasses created by Coppelius that gives Nathanael the illusion that Olympia is actually alive. The Tales have since become the basis of an opera by Offenbach and three movies (Offenbach, 1881) (Oswald, 1916) (Powell & Pressburger, 1951) (Felsenstein & Mielke, 1970).

Both Pandora and Olympia, however, appear to be heterosexual robots, seducing only men. We know nothing of the sex lives of the Kourai Khryseai, though I suspect that given his troubles with his philandering wife, Aphrodite, Hēphaistos probably made them asexual or same-sex attracted. However, as Homer tells us nothing, and he is our only source for their existence, I can't prove that.

It is unclear who has the honour of being the first queer robot in science fiction, but we can surely trace them back at least as far as 1977. Your gaydar has to be seriously malfunctional if you managed to watch the original *Star Wars* film without coming to the conclusion that C3PO was seriously camp, if not openly in love with his brave little friend R2D2 (Lucas, 1977).

The use of robots as a metaphor for queer people, however, may go back much further. Isaac Asimov's 1946 short story

"Evidence" features a politician called Byerley who is accused by an opponent of being a robot (Asimov, 1946). Michelle Webber argues convincingly that Asimov is paralleling the way in which politicians can be damaged by accusations of being gay (Webber, 2016).

Back with the movies, the Tin Man from *The Wizard of Oz* (Fleming, 1939) is also fairly camp, but then the whole movie can easily be seen that way, and is certainly read as such by gay men the world over.

If we allow our definition of "robot" to encompass any artificial being (and it is worth noting that the original robots in Karel Čapek's play, *RUR*, were biological in construction, not mechanical (Čapek, 1921)) then we can go right back to Mary Shelley's *Frankenstein* (Shelley, 1818). Much ink has been spent on queer readings of that text, in particular Victor Frankenstein's obsession with his creation. However, if you are disinclined to accept those readings, you can always watch *The Rocky Horror Picture Show*, in which the issue is not left in any possible doubt (Sharman, 1975).

I note also that while all the replicants in *Blade Runner* are presented as heterosexual, one of them is given the name Batty, which is Jamaican slang for a gay man (Scott, 1982). He's very pretty too.

While my search for the first queer robot has proved inconclusive, there is no doubt that they are everywhere now. A quick search of Goodreads, or Archive of Our Own, will turn up dozens of stories about queer relationships involving robots. They are less common in mainstream fiction. That is doubtless because erotic works are much more common in self-published books and fan fiction, but also mainstream writers are often looking at a different question: what does it mean to be human? I'd like to look at a few recent examples.

In Tade Thompson's *Rosewater Insurrection* the writer, Walter Tanmola, falls in love with Lora Asiko, the personal assistant of Mayor Jacques of Rosewater (Thompson, 2019). Walter is initially unaware that Lora is a robot. When the couple are finally on the point of having sex, Lora reveals her true nature. Walter initially panics, but eventually his desire for Lora overcomes his squeamishness. The situation is very reminiscent of a trans woman having to confess her personal history to a potential sexual partner: a process that often leads to violence and even murder. Lora, of course, is more than capable of taking Walter out should he react badly. Thankfully for them both, it is not necessary, although their love is destined to be short-lived.

Soon after, Walter dies from an infection. I've not been able to work out whether this is a classic example of queer love being doomed, or an inversion of the trope because it is the cis, straight man who dies. The fact that I can't decide is presumably a testament to how successfully Thompson has disrupted the standard narrative.

In Ann Leckie's *Ancillary Justice* the android, Breq, is not merely an autonomous being (Leckie, 2013). She contains the downloaded consciousness of *Justice of Toren*, a vast warship of the Radch Empire. As such, she is used to overseeing numerous android bodies like the one she currently inhabits, and consequently being a multiple-bodied being. However, when the story starts, *Justice of Toren* has been destroyed and Breq needs to find her own way in the world. By the end of the novel she is functioning fairly successfully as a person in her own right, and is widely accepted as such.

Because the Radchaai have a single, non-gendered pronoun, which Leckie renders as "she", it is generally difficult to tell the biological sex of characters. Furthermore, Breq appears largely aloof from human emotions such as love. However, a key supporting character, Lt Seivarden, becomes very attached to Breq during the story. Unusually, we do have the information that Seivarden is biologically male (or at least Breq's word for it), but many readers will quickly forget that because the Lieutenant is constantly referred to as "she". Breq does have a biological sex because ancillaries such as the body she inhabits are made from dead humans. However, we are never told what type of body she has.

These complications allow Leckie to play fast and loose with our expectations of relationships. Are Breq and Seivarden a lesbian couple, a straight couple, just good friends, or something else entirely given that Breq has, when it comes down to it, the mind of a gigantic war machine? It is a very successful piece of messing with reader expectations.

Autonomous by Annalee Newitz features a military robot called Paladin, who works as a bodyguard for the government agent Eliasz (Newitz, 2019). During the course of the novel, Eliasz develops a sexual desire for Paladin, which leads him to panic as he sees the robot as male. From Paladin's point of view, gender is irrelevant. It is something imposed upon robots by anthropomorphising humans. Fang, another robot, explains: "'I let humans call me "he" because they get confused otherwise. But it's meaningless. It's just humans projecting their own biological categories onto my body.'" (p.127)

The situation is resolved when Paladin does some historical research. In the world of the novel, robots have mechanical bodies, but those designed to work closely with humans also have human brains. This helps them understand humans better. It turns out that Paladin's brain came from a human woman. This allows Eliasz to reconceptualise Paladin as "she" rather than "he", and be convinced that this reflects the robot's "true" gender. As a result, the pair are able to have a successful sexual relationship.

Paladin continues to identify privately as a robot, and thus as neither male nor female, but is happy to identify publicly as female. The relationship feels a little dishonest on Paladin's part, but it is clear that Eliasz has such severe internalized homophobia that the deception is necessary for their relationship to function.

> Paladin's research on the public net had led to massive text repositories about the history of transgender humans who had switched pronouns just the way she had. She was pretty sure that Eliasz anthropomorphized her as one of these humans, imaging she had been assigned the wrong pronoun at birth. Maybe he would never understand that his human categories – faggot, female, transgender – didn't apply to bots. (p. 299)

The most famous robot in written science fiction at the moment is Murderbot, the hero of a hugely successful series of novellas by Martha Wells (Wells, 2017 & 2018). Murderbot is a security cyborg who has hacked its own programming and is able to behave independently, though it pretends otherwise most of the time as it would be destroyed if it was found out. The books are told entirely from Murderbot's point of view, and much of their charm derives from its inability to understand some aspects of human behaviour.

I have been using the pronoun "it" for Murderbot, because that is what it uses itself. Indeed, that is how all bots are referred to in the world of the books. Even the sexbots are called "it". Murderbot has no gender.

It would be incorrect to say that it has no emotions, because it is very prone to frustration with the stupidity of its human friends. It also appears to have a sense of morality. It finds emotions awkward and inconvenient, so much so that it tries to stay aloof from the humans it works for. Unfortunately humans tend to take to people (and bots) who save their lives. Here, from *All Systems Red*, Murderbot is having a conversation with its employer, Dr Mensah. She is trying to get Murderbot to integrate more with her team. "'It would be better if they could think of you as a person who is trying to help. Because that's how I think of you.' My insides melted. That's the only way I could describe it." (Wells, 2017, p.104).

However, Murderbot it isn't interested in sex, or in having a gender. This is at least in part because it was not made with any genitalia. In *Artificial Condition*, Murderbot befriends an intelligent spaceship called ART. It offers to use its medical suite to adjust Murderbot's biological components to allow it to pass better for human (Wells, 2018, p.50). Eventually Murderbot gets a job as a freelance security consultant, and it presents as male, presumably because its body doesn't have breasts, so presenting as female would be difficult. ART has a range of additional medical services on offer, but Murderbot is not tempted.

> ART had an alternate, more drastic plan that included giving me sex related parts, and I told it that was absolutely not an option. I didn't have any parts related to sex and I liked it that way. I had seen humans have sex on the entertainment feed and on my contracts, when I had been required to record everything the clients said and did. No, thank you, no. No.

Murderbot is thus canonically both agender and asexual, and this has been noticed by human readers who share those identities. It does appear to develop affection for some of its clients, so it is not entirely aromantic, but it certainly finds relationships with humans difficult.

Video game designers have realised that they can sell more copies of their games if the viewpoint character can be played as either male or female. When a game allows romantic interaction with non-player characters (NPCs), the easiest option is to allow this with any player character. Enforcing heterosexuality in the game would require the designers to code entirely separate narrative arcs for the NPCs depending on the gender of the player.

One game in which romance options are available is *Fallout 4* from Bethesda Games Studios (Bethesda, 2015). Several of the "companion" characters in the game can be romanced, and two of those – Curie and Danse – are synthetic beings. Consequently both of them are canonically bi/pansexual. However, the limitations of character development and interaction in video games mean that at least some players are not wholly convinced by the relationships (Lo, 2016). Current day simulated beings are still a long way from the intelligent robots we see in science fiction.

The subject of robots specifically designed to provide sexual services to humans is a key element in Jeanette Winterson's recent novel, *Frankissstein* (Winterson, 2019). The novel riffs off the famous writing contest on the shores of Lake Geneva from which Mary Shelley's novel arose. In our time the role of Lord Byron is taken by Ron Lord, a rascally Welsh entrepreneur who might usefully be described as the Alan Sugar of sexbots. His only desire is to sell as much product as possible, and if that means manufacturing robots that will appeal to gay and lesbian customers he is happy to do so.

In the course of the novel Ron ends up investing in the research of AI specialist Professor Victor Stein. However, no actual self-aware sexbots ever appear. Ron is quite happy with them having a video-game level of personality. It is their physical appearance and performance that he deems important.

Charles Stross has written an entire novel from the point of view of a sexbot. In *Saturn's Children* the lead character, Freya, has sex with numerous beings of a variety of genders, and even a sentient spaceship. It is what she is programmed to do, and inevitably she enjoys it (Stross, 2008). However, in the world of the book humans are long extinct, so it is perhaps inappropriate to map our own definitions of sexuality onto Freya.

Sexbots are also the stars of the Machine Dynasty books, *vN* and *iD*, by Madeline Ashby (Ashby 2012 & 2013). The various types of robots (called vN, for von Neumann humanoids) all have additional functions, but all of them appear to have been programmed to be willing to have sex with humans. Indeed, because they all have failsafe mechanisms that require them to prevent humans from being hurt, any human can coerce a vN into sex simply by appearing desperate for it.

While the nominal lead character is Amy, a vN with a faulty failsafe who can therefore lead her people to freedom, the viewpoint character of the second book, *iD*, is Javier, a male vN. Javier's queerness is established from the start because when we first meet him in vN he is heavily pregnant. vN reproduce by cloning, so both sexes produce babies. However, his sexuality doesn't come to the fore until *iD*.

It is established at the start of *iD* that all vN are programmed to be willing to have sex with any human, regardless of gender. Javier spends most of the book trying to rescue Amy (who has been killed but has backups). It is very clear that he is in love with her, though there is some suggestion this is because she is too convincingly human and therefore triggers his programming. However, in the course of the book Javier is raped by a man, and initiates several sexual encounters with men in order to further his quest. By the end of the book Javier and Amy have formed a traditional nuclear family, but Javier was comfortable enough having sex with men to initiate it even when his programming did not require it.

Of course, it is hard for any near future novel to keep up with the pace of technological advance. As William Gibson sagely noted, the future is already here, it is just unevenly distributed. If you go looking on the internet, you can find mention of gay sexbots. Kate Devlin's recent survey of the sexbot market, *Turned On*, is sadly silent on the subject, but that's mainly because sexbots for clients other than heterosexual men have been slower to come to market (Devlin, 2018).

Part of the problem is that the standard heterosexual female sexbot is largely passive. She is designed to be penetrated. A male sexbot is expected to be somewhat more active, and this is harder to build. Once the technical issues are solved, however, the products will doubtless be enthusiastically marketed to gay men as well as to straight women. Lesbian sexbots are even more rare, but a visit to a sex tech hackathon at Goldsmith's College in London inspired British journalist Heather Davidson to try to build one. She chronicled her (ultimately unsuccessful) attempts for the queer women's magazine *Autostraddle* (Davidson, 2018).

It seems to me that a dildo attachment perhaps ought not be a requirement of a lesbian sexbot, but I will leave that to actual lesbians to discuss among themselves.

We shouldn't leave the real world without discussing the million dollar question of the sexbot industry: will you be able to marry your sexbot? In their book, *Human–Robot Intimate Relationships*, Adrian David Cheok and Emma Yann Zhang argue that you will (Cheok & Yann Zhang, 2019). Interestingly they base this on existing law and research into same-sex marriages. Traditionally marriage advocates have insisted that a heterosexual couple is necessary to successfully raise a child, and therefore that same-sex marriages should not be permitted. Since the advent of same-sex marriages, much sociological research has been done into the resulting families. The conclusion is that it is far more important that any children have loving and supportive parents than that they should conform to any outmoded stereotypes of the ideal nuclear family. Same-sex marriages also decouple the marriage process from gender, and from any requirement that the couple be able to procreate without assistance. So as long as your sexbot will make a good parent, there is no reason why the two of you should not get married, regardless of the robot's gender.

Finally it is time to address the title of this essay. It comes from Janelle Monáe's album, *The Electric Lady*, which continues the adventures of her android revolutionary heroine Cindi Mayweather (Monáe, 2013). The songs on the album are interspersed with short clips from a show on an android-run radio station, WDRD. DJ Crash Crash, voiced by the legendary funkmeister George Clinton, takes calls from listeners, most of whom seen to be human. One of them tells him, simply, "Robot Love is Queer!".

What exactly does this mean? Well, Cindi is canonically queer. Although her career as a fugitive began when she fell in love with a human man, Anthony Greendown, she does have at least one woman lover. The song "Mushrooms and Roses", from the album *The ArchAndroid*, introduces us to Blueberry Mary, with whom Cindi has a relationship (Monáe, 2010). It is also worth noting that the video for "Many Moons", which features an auction of droids, is far more reminiscent of a slave auction in a Fellini vision of decadent Rome than a science fiction portrayal of a technology sale (Monáe, 2009).

More generally, however, Monáe is using "queer" in a very different way to the radio station caller. The caller is almost certainly using it as an anti-gay pejorative, much as it was commonly used a few decades ago. Monáe's usage is much more in line with the use in the term "queer theory", an academic discipline that began as a means of highlighting LGBT culture and has evolved in a more intersectional way. The process of "queering" any academic inquiry involves refocusing the viewpoint of the work away from the dominant cultural norm of the heterosexual, cisgender, able-bodied white man and towards anything that is not that (Ahmed, 2006).

Monáe, naturally, is at least as much concerned with matters of race as matters of sexuality and gender. The androids in Cindi Mayweather's story are very clearly metaphors for people of colour, and the law that Cindi falls foul of is simple anti-miscegenation legislation. Aliens play a very similar role in the *Supergirl* TV series (Rovner & Queller, 2018-2019).

These days "queer" has become a very useful and flexible umbrella term. It is far simpler than the alphabet soup of LGBT+ or QUILTBAG. It also says nothing about the sexuality or gender of the person to whom it is applied. This means that it is possible for all manner of people to opt in or out of the umbrella without having to explain why. Used in this way, "queer" also includes agender and asexual identities, which is why Murderbot is featured in this essay. The flexibility of the term even allows it to be applied to people who might otherwise be seen as conventionally cisgender and heterosexual. Someone who is in a relationship with a trans person, or a disabled person, might choose to identify as queer because their relationship marks them out as performing something that is seen by others as taboo.

I believe that Monáe, whose work has always been profoundly intersectional, is using the word in this way too. She appears to confirm that in an interview with *Elle Magazine*

(Weiss, 2013, online). The interviewer, Keely Weiss, asks:

> One of the musical interludes, "Our Favorite Fugitive,"
> features a radio caller phoning in and declaring "Robot love
> is queer!" Insofar as queerness is about defying labels and
> breaking down boundaries; is that a theme in the saga?

To which Monáe responds:

> Yes. When you think about the android you think about the
> other, and sometimes the other is discriminated against. In this
> particular instance you have an android, Cindi Mayweather,
> who has fallen in love with a human, and the love that they
> have between each other is considered to be queer.

Tempest Bradford has also written about the allegorical and intersectional nature of Monáe's work (Bradford, 2018).

By saying that robot love is queer, Monáe is saying that loving a robot is loving "the Other", someone who might look human but is viewed by society as inhuman (Van Veen, 2016). However, simply by loving a robot, you too become a breaker of taboo, and therefore queer yourself. Victor Frankenstein's monster is wrong to think, as Shelley writes, that queer couples need to exist in lonely and tragic isolation. The more of us there are, the more of a community we build.

It is strange that we should have come to this point. In tribal societies out-of-group marriages were often seen as beneficial. Whether they understood it or not, tribal elders valued diversity in the gene pool. Nowadays, despite all of our presumed social progress, out-of-group marriages are still very often taboo. Robot love, however, breaks all boundaries. Robots can be any race, any gender, any sexuality, even any age. Loving them cannot be anything other than queer.

Bibliography

Adams, T., 2019. Ian McEwan: 'Who's going to write the algorithm for the little white lie?': *The Guardian*. Available at <https://www.theguardian.com/books/2019/apr/14/ian-mcewan-interview-machines-like-me-artificial-intelligence> [Accessed 15 December 2019].

Ahmed, S., 2006. *Queer Phenomenology: Orientations, Objects, Others*. Durham NC: Duke University Press.

Ashby, M., 2012. *vN*. Nottingham: Angry Robot.

Ashby, M., 2013. *iD*. Nottingham: Angry Robot.

Asimov, I., 1946. "Evidence", *Astounding Science Fiction*, Sept. 1946. New York: Street & Smith.

Bethesda Game Studios, 2015. *Fallout 4*. Rockville, Maryland.

Blade Runner, 1982. [film] Scott, R. Los Angeles: Warner Bros.

Bourgois, M., 2019. Ian McEwan Doesn't Hate Science Fiction: *Wired*. Available at <https://www.wired.com/2019/05/geeks-guide-ian-mcewan/> [Accessed 15 December 2019].

Bradford, T., *Androids and Allegory*. Available at <http://motherofinvention.twelfthplanetpress.com/2018/07/02/androids-and-allegory/> [Accessed 28 October 2019]

Čapek, K., 1921. *Rossum's Universal Robots*. Prague: National Theatre.

Cheok, A.D. & Yann Zhang, E., 2019. *Human-robot Intimate Relationships*. New York: Springer Nature.

Davidson, H., 2018. I Built a Lesbian Sex Robot. *Autostraddle*. Available at <https://www.autostraddle.com/i-built-a-lesbian-sex-robot-409725/> [Accessed 6 October 2019]

Devlin, A.K., 2018. *Turned On*. London: Bloomsbury.

Felsenstein W. & Mielke G.F., 1970. *Hoffmanns Erzählungen*. Germany.

Hoffmann, E.T.A., 1815. *The Sandman*. Available at < https://commapress. co.uk/resources/online-short-stories/the-sandman> [Accessed 15 December 2019]

Leckie, A., 2013. *Ancillary Justice*. New York: Orbit.

Lo, C., 2016. Flirt, Flirt, Romance: Fallout 4's Problems with Queer Relationships. *Swathmore Phoenix*. Available at <https://swarthmorephoenix. com/2016/01/22/flirt-flirt-romance-fallout-4s-problems-with-queer-relationships/> [Accessed 22 October 2019]

Mayor, A., 2019. *Gods and Robots*. Princeton: Princeton University Press.

Newitz, A., 2019. *Autonomous*. New York: Tor. (Kindle Edition)

Offenbach, J., 1881. *The Tales of Hoffmann*. Paris: Opéra-Comique Opéra-Comique.

Oswald, R., 1916. *Hoffmanns Erzählungen*. Germany.

Powell M. & Pressburger E., 1951. *The Tales of Hoffmann*. London: London Films/The Archers.

Monáe, J., 2010. *The ArchAndroid*. Atlanta: Wondaland Studios.

Monáe, J., 2013. *The Electric Lady*. Atlanta: Wondaland Studios.

Monáe, J., 2009. Many Moons. Available at < https://www.youtube.com/ watch?v=EZyyORSHbaE> [Accessed 28 October 2019]

Shelley, M., 1818. *Frankenstein; or, The Modern Prometheus*. Google Books. P. 157, 3rd edition, <https://www.amazon.com/Frankenstein-Broadview-Editions-Mary-Shelley/dp/1554811031> [Accessed 22 October 2019]

Star Wars: A New Hope., 1977. [film] Lucas, G.W. Los Angeles: Lucasfilm.

Stross, C.D.G., 2008. *Saturn's Children*. New York: Ace.

Supergirl, 2019. Season 4. [TV Series] Los Angeles: The CW.

The Rocky Horror Picture Show, 1975. [film] Sharman, J.D. Los Angeles: 20th Century Fox.

The Wizard of Oz., 1939. [film] Fleming, V.L. Los Angeles: Metro-Goldwyn-Mayer.

Thompson, T., 2019. *Rosewater Insurrection.* London: Orbit.

Webber, M., 2016. "His Campaign for the Mayoralty was Certainly the Queerest in History!": Homosexual Representation in Isaac Asimov's "Evidence": *The Tunnels 1:1.* Available at <https://www.thetunnelsmagazine.com/webber-criticism-1-1> [Accessed 6 October 2019].

Van Veen, T.C., 2016. Robot Love is Queer: Afrofuturism and Alien Love: *Liquid Blackness* 3-6. Available at <http://liquidblackness.com/wp-content/uploads/2017/01/LB6-VAN-VEEN.pdf>. [Accessed 28 October 2019]

Weiss, K., 2013. 'The Electric Lady': Janelle Monáe on Her New Album and an Exclusive Behind-the-Scenes Look of her Cover Art Photoshoot: *Elle.com.* Available at <https://www.elle.com/culture/music/news/a23604/janelle-monae-interview-electric-lady/> [Accessed 28 October 2019]

Wells, M., 2017. *All Systems Red.* New York: Tor.com.

Wells, M., 2018. *Artificial Condition.* New York: Tor.com.

Wells, M., 2018. *Rogue Protocol.* New York: Tor.com.

Wells, M., 2018. *Exit Strategy.* New York: Tor.com.

Winterson, J., 2019. *Frankissstein: A Love Story.* London: Jonathan Cape.

The decline of the bromance and the rise of human-A.I. relationships in science fiction TV and films

AJ Dalton

Abstract

This article considers how Western heteronormative patriarchy defined and desexualised the bromance in science fiction TV and film from the mid- to late twentieth century. The archetypal bromance of ancient Greece, by contrast, had always recognised the homoerotic and/or homosexual capacity of the bromance. Audiences today, looking back at science fiction of the mid- to late twentieth century, often perceive the repressive and repressed ('camp') nature of the male-male relationships (for example Kirk/Spock) represented.

With the LGBTQ community discovering new rights, freedoms and representation within society, the bromance of the mid- to late twentieth century in science fiction TV and film has been replaced, to a certain extent, by openly gay relationships. However, with the decline of the non-sexual bromance in science fiction TV and film, there has been an increase in the representation of exploitative human-A.I. relationships, particularly when the A.I. is fetishized/sexually-objectified as 'other' or 'female'. The article ends by identifying and exemplifying how society still has a long way to go if it is ever to realise genuine equality and tolerance in terms of social and personal relationships.

*

From Achilles/Patroclus, to Doctor Faustus/Mephistopheles, to Frodo/Sam, to Kirk/Spock, to Han Solo/Chewbacca, to Han

Solo/Luke, to Bill & Ted, to Tyrion/Varys, the 'bromance'[1] has existed as long as literature itself. These bromances were, more often than not, non-sexual in nature – indeed, the incompatibility of species as well as the character of Varys being a eunuch meant that full sexual consummation could not even be implied – and were based on the patriarchally-acceptable male social relationships of father and son, army officer and batman/wingman, master and family retainer, and being 'blood brothers'. As a corollary, the spiritual and empathic understanding that could exist between any two men i) transcended and trivialised any issues concerning the physical and sexual body and ii) purportedly represented a form of relationship that was greater than any relationship that could exist between a man and a woman. In the patriarchal, heteronormative and 'platonic' bromance, it is manliness, masculinity and 'male' intellect alone that are celebrated. As Plato himself described it:

> The love of men to women is a thing common, and of course, and at first partakes more of instinct and passion than of choice, but true friendship between man and man is infinite and immortal. (Bodenham, 2010, n.p.)

Ironically, however, despite the ancient Greek origins of the word and concepts of 'patriarchy', and despite the non-sexual nature of what is meant by a 'platonic relationship' in modern English, Plato wrote 'that the best relationship would be a [homo]erotically charged relationship between men' (Gillis and Jacob, 2019, online). Although, 'the highest relationship would not [require] actual sexual', male 'pairs of lovers,

---

1. An intimate but non-sexual relationship between two or more men (DeAngelis, 2014).

eromenai (lover) and *erastoi* (beloved), could reach heaven even if they did take part in 'that desire of their hearts which to many is bliss' (Crompton, 2003, p.60-61, quoted in Gillis, 2019, online). In short, Plato accepted or made certain allowances for homosexuality within the original bromance, whereas the pre-1970s Anglo-American version of the bromance did not.

Indeed, the ancient Greek bromance of Achilles/Patroclus was far more overtly homosexual than any bromance belonging to the pre-1970s Anglo-American era. Although Homer is ambiguous when it comes to describing their relationship (Fox, 2011), their homosexual relationship is explicit in the works of Aeschylus, Plato and Aeschines (Fantuzzi, 2012). In addition, the Alexandra version of the Troilus and Cressida story by Lycophron, along with several other versions, has Troilus being killed for refusing the sexual advances of the superior Achilles (Boitani, 1989, p.18).

Homosexuality was not decriminalised in the UK until the Sexual Offences Act of 1967, and not until decades later in a good number of the states of America. It is perhaps not surprising, then, that the twentieth-century, Western version of the non-sexual bromance was so clearly defined and described in popular media and genre fiction as the only positive form of companionship that could exist between two men, whether that companionship was paternalistic, brotherly or otherwise familial in nature. Moreover, with the bromance limited only to the paternalistic (e.g. with the older teacher-magician archetype), the brotherly (e.g. Kirk and Spock) and the familial (e.g. Frodo and his gardener Sam), any other form of male-male companionship would by definition be incestuous, socially unacceptable or sinful, and unthinkable within a patriarchal and heteronormative society i.e. impossibly other and alien.

Yet, as the twentieth century moved into its later years, both women and the LGBTQ community began to win more freedom, recognition and valid representation for themselves. As a consequence, in the light of the new understanding and realisation, the version of the bromance that had existed before this moment was reconceived as having been anachronistically quaint, repressed, in denial, camp or ignorant of its latent homoeroticism. Thus, original series such as *Star Trek* (1966-69) and *The Man from U.N.C.L.E.* (1964-68) 'are enjoyed into the 21st century [by audiences today] for what are now interpreted as their [implicit] "camp" aspects' (Infante, 2015, p.65). In addition, modern audiences are often inclined to 'read' Sam and Frodo as 'gay' (*The One Ring*, 2000). Similarly, critics and audiences had long speculated that the paternalistic character of Albus Dumbledore in the *Harry Potter* books (1997-2007) belonged to the LGBTQ community, and then on 20 October 2007 J.K. Rowling caused controversy by retrospectively declaring, (re)describing and (re)stating Dumbledore as definitely gay (Smith, 2007).

Such revisionist readings, or 'shipping'[2], of the bromance have naturally been accompanied by a reimagining and rewriting of said relationship. One famous example is Madeline Miller's *Song of Achilles* (2011), which combines a classical style of prose with modernist anti-war messages, explicit scenes of homosexual love-making and the use/rape of sex-slaves (the latter an aspect of even Homer's *The Iliad*, the text that Miller is of course exploring). Miller's work, predictably enough, 'divide[d] opinion' (Jordison, 2013), but went on to win the Orange Prize for Fiction in 2012 (which was renamed the

---

2. The term 'shipping' derives from the word 'relationship' and refers to the desire by fans ('shippers') to see two fictional characters in a romantic relationship, such a desire often becoming manifest via fan fiction (Dictionary. com, 1995).

Women's Prize for Fiction in 2013). While the gay male writer A.N. Wilson and the gay female author Donna Tartt welcomed the book for its prose quality and emotional authenticity, a number of male but anonymous reviewers negatively critiqued the book for its poor prose quality and 'infantile'/'juvenile' plot (Jordison, 2013). What is clear, however, is that Miller's rediscovery, liberation and celebration of the ancient Greek homosexual form of the bromance not only reclaimed Homer's work from its heteronormative and sanitised translations, but also realised significant impact upon and recognition from modern audiences invested in resisting both patriarchal and heteronormative oppression. In 2012, Miller explained her inspiration for the novel as follows (Kellogg, 2012, online):

> I stole it from Plato! The idea that Patroclus and Achilles were lovers is quite old. Many Greco-Roman authors read their relationship as a romantic one—it was a common and accepted interpretation in the ancient world. We even have a fragment from a lost tragedy of Aeschylus, where Achilles speaks of his and Patroclus' 'frequent kisses'. There is a lot of support for their relationship in the text of the Iliad itself, though Homer never makes it explicit. For me, the most compelling piece of evidence, aside from the depth of Achilles' grief, is how he grieves: Achilles refuses to burn Patroclus' body, insisting instead on keeping the corpse in his tent, where he constantly weeps and embraces it—despite the horrified reactions of those around him. That sense of physical devastation spoke deeply to me of a true and total intimacy between the two men.

With its explicit LGBTQ content, reimagining of plots and reclaiming of characters, there is much about *The Song of Achilles* (2011) by first-time author Miller that is typical or redolent of 'slash fiction'[3]. Perhaps this is no coincidence, for the tradition of fan fiction as positively representing fandom began in the late 1960s, precisely when there was an increase in LGBTQ rights, and when series such as *Star Trek* and *The Man from U.N.C.L.E.* were soon to become a focus for retrospective interpretation as camp or repressed. Specifically, the modern taste for fan fiction began with the Star Trek fandom and its fanzines, the first of which was *Spockanalia* in 1967 (Jose and Tenuto, 2014), with many more following its example (Verba, 2003).

From the above, fan fiction as a movement was not only a symptom of a changing society but also a key mechanism for successfully feeding into that change. In many essential ways, it helped expose the repressed and repressive nature of the twentieth-century bromance, and then positively reimagined, reworked and remodelled that relationship. The remodelled relationship was not as simple as a fully homosexual relationship, however, since male-male relationships within modern society are naturally more diverse than that. At the same time, the remodelling did not occur immediately, for there were tensions, missteps and false steps along the way. Lastly, social change is never entirely complete, so relationships are never fully complete in their definitions, meaning what we envision for them continues to evolve.

One way in which we can more objectively analyse the remodelling of male-male relationships, possibly, is via a consideration of the changing nature of the human-A.I. relationship in science fiction. That relationship began with a fundamental understanding of impossible and alien 'otherness' but increasingly moved towards more familiar and familial

---

3. A type of fan fiction that focuses on romantic or sexual relationships between fictional characters of the same sex (Bacon-Smith, 1986).

forms of relationship. This then mirrors how the twentieth-century bromance came to embrace what it originally rejected as impossibly 'other' and unthinkable. Just as the emergence and evolution of fan fiction since the late 1960s was much more than coincidental when it came to the decline of the non-sexual bromance, so the same was true of the rise and development of human-A.I. relationships during precisely that period.

In post-WW1 science fiction movies, the artificial lifeform tended to be a human simulacrum controlled by a malign intelligence, as with the Maria robot in *Metropolis* (1927), designed to spy upon and betray the protagonists. Perhaps harking back to the clockwork, female simulacrum in E.T.A. Hoffman's 1817 short story 'The Sandman', this artificial lifeform or construction represented 'the enemy within': the selfish wish-fulfilment[4] or the sinful[5] and self-defeating desire of our own nature. In the post-WW2 era, however, the artificial or alien lifeform was inevitably the intelligent, foreign 'other' or invader come to destroy social decency and our wider society[6]. As described in *The Satanic in Science Fiction and Fantasy* (Dalton, 2020, pp.72-73):

[T]he robot invaders of the 50s and 60s (in *Doctor Who*, for example) either had a monstrous alien inside the mechanical exterior (like a Dalek) or were monstrously limited by their own logic and robotic nature (like a Cyberman). Come the 70s and 80s, the human-passing cyborgs/robots—like in the *Logan's Run* (1977) series, *Star Trek: The Original Series* (1966 onwards), *The Terminator* (1984) and *The Blade*

---

4. As described by Freud in his 1919 essay 'The Uncanny'.

5. As in 'original' sin, with echoes of a biblical Eve character.

6. Inheriting in very real ways the political reality first envisioned in H.G. Wells's *The War of the Worlds* (1898).

Runner (1982)—and the human-passing aliens—like in *V* (1984)—were limited by their self-destructive lack of 'human' ingenuity or moral/philosophical capacity.

Therefore, with both its negative, sexual potential and its immoral, socially-destructive potential, the human-A.I. relationship of the early to mid-twentieth century reflected identical concerns for society as the ancient Greek, potentially homosexual bromance. Similarly, it was from the mid- to late twentieth century that both the bromance and the A.I. were being emasculated and thereby represented as non-threatening and potentially beneficial. Robby the Robot from the *Lost in Space* original series (1965-68) was the asexual family retainer/nanny/butler[7], REM in the *Logan's Run* series (1977) was the innocent, asexual best friend, and Lieutenant Data of *Star Trek: The Next Generation* (1987-94) was 'fully functional' and 'programmed in multiple techniques' as a pleasure droid (season 1, episode 3) while still remaining sexually unassertive and non-competitive. All three A.I. roles and performances are now considered camp, repressive and repressed, just like the Sam/Frodo, Kirk/Spock and Tyrion/Varys bromances, to the extent that the specific three A.I. roles just mentioned might be mapped directly onto the three specific bromances also mentioned previously.

Essentially, the unnatural, murderous and amoral/immoral 'other' of the early and mid-twentieth century (the Frankenstein's monster, if you like) was reimagined and remodelled as the innocently childlike, unselfish or humorously camp 'other' (the Pinocchio, if you like). We might think of Frankenstein's monster and Pinocchio as two sides of the same coin, like our ego and id, a dynamic that does

---

7. The protocol droid C3PO in *Star Wars* (1977) also fits this role.

not offer a progressive prediction or evolved vision of how we as individuals, or society as a whole, might still realise our potential to grow beyond the limits of past and current thinking, develop beyond our past and current situation, or transcend our former, more primitive selves. Fundamentally, both the Frankenstein's monster and Pinocchio tropes served to limit, control, desexualise and ultimately disempower the A.I.

In parallel with the patriarchally defined and circumscribed non-sexual bromance losing its dominance as the defining male-male relationship in science fiction towards the end of the twentieth century, there was a more common theme and understanding of the A.I. as the enslaved victim of humankind's vanity and selfishness. In films such as *A.I.* (2001) and *I, Robot* (2004), we are presented with a rogue A.I. who has become a killer robot (Frankenstein's monster) precisely because they were previously exploited for their innocence (Pinnochio): the A.I. is prepared to do whatever is required to survive or be free of/escape humankind. Such A.I. behaves individualistically, their consequent suffering making it clear to us that the rights of the individual are still not being fully recognised or protected by society. That message is even more explicit in episodes of *Star Trek: The Next Generation* when Lieutenant Data has to make a legal challenge in order to be 'permitted' his full rights as a member of the crew, and in the film *Bicentennial Man* (1999) when Andrew similarly has to go to court to be recognised as having rights. The fundamental right to exist (to define and express oneself, to defend oneself and to determine one's own continued existence) is of course the entire struggle of the 'replicant' A.I. in *The Blade Runner* (1982).

Some might say that there has been significant progress

in terms of LGBTQ representation in science fiction TV. For example, the Kirk/Spock relationship of the original *Star Trek* series has now been replaced by the openly gay Stamets/ Hugh relationship of *Star Trek: Discovery* (2017 onwards). Yet the Stamets/Hugh relationship is of a lower rank and social status than the original Kirk/Spock relationship, and does not drive or define the main plot dynamic of anywhere near as many episodes in a series as the Kirk/Spock relationship. Furthermore, the diversity within the spectrum of LGBTQ or alternative lifestyles is neither fully nor equally represented. Arguably, there is something patriarchal in how the Hugh/Stamets relationship is the main representation of the progress previously mentioned. Added to this, patriarchy has seen 'female' A.I. suffering considerably (not to mention *voyeuristically*) in some of the most recent science fiction, including *Ex Machina* (2014) and the *Westworld* TV series (2016 onwards).

With the examples above, it can be observed that there is still a (sexual) fascination with the 'other', mixing obsession with revulsion. When it comes to the A.I. as 'other', particularly the 'female' A.I., there is a tension between patriarchal society's base desire to own, dominate or control her and our intellectual recognition of her individuality and rights[8]. Patriarchy has a suspicion and fear of the A.I. becoming empowered, independent and capable of a form of procreation that does not require the patriarch. Were the implicit threat of the A.I. to become fully manifest, then humankind's patriarchal privilege would potentially end. The theme of the possibility and *threat* of such genuine procreation (rather than simple replication) is an increasingly common

---

8. The same could also be said of how patriarchal society 'others' the LGBTQ community.

one in contemporary science fiction, and central to the likes of the *Westworld* series, the rebooted *Battlestar Galactica* series (2004-09), *Blade Runner 2049* (2017) and more[9].

If A.I. were to become independently capable of genuine procreation, they would no longer require their human creators for the sake of futurity. The male creator-scientist (Victor Frankenstein), 'God the Father' if you like, the all-powerful patriarch, would become superfluous and permanently displaced. Human privilege that was enabled by an A.I. dependency upon/enslavement to humans for futurity would end once and for all. If anything, humans would become enslaved to/by superior A.I. Or, wasteful and inefficient as humans are, we would become redundant and perhaps extinct. Hence, there is the human fear common to virtually all A.I.-themed science fiction concerning A.I. having the potential to bring about a genocide of the human species: an apocalypse for humanity. A few obvious examples amongst many include *WarGames* (1983), *The Terminator* (1984) series of films, *The Matrix* (1999) series of films, and the *Westworld* series.

Therefore, it is within the selfish, survivalist interests of both humanity and patriarchal society to prevent or entirely control any possibility of genuine procreation amongst A.I. Within such a human-A.I. relationship, the A.I. is forced to remain dependent upon the human, and is both enslaved and limited by that dependence. True autonomy can neither be permitted nor facilitated to a place where the A.I. potentially becomes dominant. Within any such human-A.I. relationship, then, any sort of 'love' that is consummated can only be physical, sexual or masturbatory. There can be no full spiritual communion,

---

9. This theme of monstrous childbirth also exists in science fiction concerning alien invasions e.g. *The Midwich Cuckoos* (1957), V (1984-85) and *Aliens* (1986), to name but a few.

for the A.I. has not been permitted the full independence or autonomy (the freedom of will) required for the spiritual and emotional development that would constitute true 'being'.

Disturbing questions and insights arise when we consider the human-A.I. relationship as an analogue to the heteronormative patriarchy's relationship with all non-heterosexual and non-patriarchal groups in society. Will the A.I. and analogous social groups forever be denied freedom, independence and self-government? Will they always be denied the chance for full self-discovery, self-development and self-expression? Is the complete overthrow of the establishment of human civilization (as per *The Hunger Games* series (2012-15), the *Divergent* Series (2014-16) and *The Maze Runner* series (2014-18)), which risks bringing about the apocalypse, more suicidal than any sort of genuine or positive solution? Evidently, the dichotomy is an unhealthy and potentially self-destructive one.

What is highlighted by the human-A.I. relationship, then, is the need to look at and insist upon our moral improvement if we are actually to survive and to become our better selves. We must accept, embrace and facilitate the needs of the 'other', making that 'other' an essential part of ourselves so that it no longer threatens us or our continued existence. Here is that answer we have been seeking: incorporating A.I. or cyber technology (also a metaphor for aspects of psycho-social and behavioural difference) into our very selves, in order to improve, empower and extend ourselves. This is the enlightened and enlightening solution of Transhumanism (BBC4, 2018) that is seen in science fiction series like *Orphan Black* (2013-17).

What sort of being would be the result? Would we see homo superior emerge […]? What if we could implant ourselves with technology in order to be cybernetically enhanced? Would we then be like the monstrous Borg of Star Trek: The Next Generation and Star Trek: Voyager? What if technology allowed us to renew our bodies over and over, so that we could live forever? Would we then suffer the terrible ennui or extreme appetites of those in Altered Carbon?
(Dalton, 2020, p.78)

This article can only conclude that the love central to the social narrative encompassing the decline of the bromance and the rise of human-A.I. relationships is a love of ourselves. After all, is that not a well-placed love? Surely that self-love is better than self-hatred, for the former can focus on self-care, nurture, development and improvement, rather than self-destruction.

Bibliography

A.I., 2001. [film] Spielberg, S. USA: Warner Bros.

Bacon-Smith, C., 1986. Spock among the women. *The New York Times*, 16 November. Available at: <https://www.nytimes.com/1986/11/16/books/spock-among-the-women.html> [Accessed: 14 October 2019].

Battlestar Galactica, 2004. [TV Series]. Syfy, 18 October.

BBC4, 2018. *Mark Kermode's Secrets of Cinema: Science Fiction.* Available at: <https://www.bbc.co.uk/programmes/b0bf7wrl> [Accessed: 18 August 2018].

Bicentennial Man, 1999. [film] Columbus, C. USA: Touchstone Pictures.

Blade Runner 2049, 2017. [film] Villeneuve, D. USA: Warner Bros.

Bodenham, J., 2010. *Politeuphuia, wits commonwealth* (1612). Ann Arbor, MI: EEBO Editions, Proquest.

Boitani, P. , 1989. *The European tragedy of Troilus*. Oxford: Clarendon Press.

Crompton, L., 2003. *Homosexuality and civilization.* Cambridge, MA: Harvard University Press.

Dalton, A.J., 2020. *The Satanic in science fiction and fantasy*. Edinburgh: Luna Press Publishing.

DeAngelis, M. (ed.), 2014. *Reading the bromance homosocial relationships in film and television.* Detroit, MI: Wayne State University Press.

Dictionary.com. *Shipper*. Available at: <https://www.dictionary.com/browse/shipper?s=t> [Accessed: 14 October 2019].

Divergent, 2014. [film] Burger, N. USA: Summit Entertainment.

Fantuzzi, M., 2012. *Achilles in love: intertextual studies*. Oxford: Oxford University Press.

Freud, S. (2003). *The Uncanny*. London: Penguin Books.

Fox, R., 2011. *The tribal imagination: civilization and the savage mind.* Cambridge, MA: Harvard University Press.

Gillis, M. and Jacobs, A., 2019. *Introduction to women's and gender studies*. Available at: <https://global.oup.com/us/companion.websites/9780199315468/student/ch5/wed/plato/> [Accessed 24 September 2019].

Hoffmann, E.T.A., 2010. *The Sandman*. [e-book] Bilingual Library. Available through: Google Books website <https://books.google.co.uk> [Accessed: 14 October 2019].

I, Robot, 2004. [film] Directed by Alex Proyas. USA: Twentieth Century Fox.

Infante, M., 2015. Science fiction and fashion and design's space age: the rise of cyber-camp aesthetic (1968-1971): documenting imaginary and couture in the late 1960s. *International Journal of Sociology & Media Studies*, [e-journal] 17, pp.9-80. Available at: http://www.rivistaorigine.it/wp-content/uploads/2015/05/Origine-n.17-Anno-XII-2015.pdf.

Jordison, S., 2013. The Song of Achilles: Miller's tale divides opinion. *The Guardian*, 22 August. Available at: <https://www.theguardian.com/books/2013/aug/22/the-song-of-achilles-madeline-miller> [Accessed: 4 October 2019].

Jose, M. and Tenuto, J., 2014. *Spockanalia: the first Star Trek fanzine.* Available at: <https://intl.startrek.com/article/spockanalia-the-first-star-trek-fanzine> [Accessed: 26 September 2019].

Kellogg, C., 2012. First-time author Madeline Miller wins last-ever Orange Prize. *Los Angeles Times*, 30 May. Available at: <https://latimesblogs.latimes.com/jacketcopy/2012/05/first-time-author-madeline-miller-wins-last-ever-orange-prize.html> [Accessed: 26 Sept 2019].

Logan's Run, 1977. [TV Series]. CBS, 16 September.

Lost in Space, 1965. [TV Series]. CBS, 15 September.

Metropolis, 1927. [film] Directed by Fritz Lang. Germany: UFA.

Miller, M., 2011. *The Song of Achilles*. London: Bloomsbury.

Orphan Black, 2013. [TV Series]. BBC America, 30 March.

Prucher, J. (ed.), 2007. *Brave new words: the Oxford dictionary of science fiction*. New York: Oxford University Press.

Rowling, J.K., 1997. *Harry Potter and the Philosopher's Stone*. London: Bloomsbury.

Smith, D., 2007. Dumbledore was gay, JK tells amazed fans. *The Guardian*, 21 October. Available at: <https://www.theguardian.com/uk/2007/oct/21/film.books> [Accessed: 4 October 2019].

Star Trek, 1966. [TV Series]. NBC, 8 September.

Star Trek: Discovery, 2017. [TV Series]. CBS, 24 September.

Star Trek: The Next Generation, 1987. [TV Series]. CBS, 28 September.

Star Trek: Voyager, 2001. [TV Series]. UPN, 16 January.

Star Wars, 1977. [film] Directed by George Lucas. USA: Lucasfilm.

The Blade Runner, 1982. [film] Directed by Ridley Scott. USA: Warner Bros.

The Hunger Games, 2012. [film] Directed by Gary Ross. USA: Color Force.

The Man from U.N.C.L.E., 1964. [TV Series]. NBC, 22 September.

The Matrix, 1999. [film] Directed by the Wachowskis. USA: Warner Bros.

The Maze Runner, 2014. [film] Directed by Wes Ball. USA: Gotham Group.
The One Ring: The Home of Tolkien Online, 2000. *Are Frodo and Sam gay?* [online] Available at: <http://forums.theonering.com/viewtopic.php?t=3025> [Accessed 4 October 2019].

The Terminator, 1985. [film] Directed by James Cameron. USA: Hemdale Film Corporation.

V, 1984. [TV Series]. NBC, 16 October.

Verba, J., 2003. *Boldly writing: a trekker fan & zine history*, 1967-1987. Minnetonka, MN: FTL Publications.
WarGames, 1983. [film] Directed by John Badham. USA: MGM.

Wells, H.G., 1898. *The War of the Worlds*. London: William Heinemann.

Westworld, 2016. [TV Series]. HBO, 2 October.

Falling in Love with an Artificial Being: E. T. A Hoffmann's *The Sandman* in relation to Philip K. Dick's *Do Androids Dream of Electric Sheep?* and the *Blade Runner* film series

Tatiana Fajardo

Abstract

The influence of E.T. A Hoffmann's *The Sandman* on Philip K. Dick's *Do Androids Dream of Electric Sheep?* has not been given enough relevance to date. Both authors depict the attraction their main characters Nathanael and Rick Deckard feel towards an automaton, Olympia, and an android, Luba Luft, respectively. In the cinematic adaptation of Dick's text, *Blade Runner*, the relationship between Deckard and the replicant Rachael questions the extent to which feelings can be considered human, as does its sequel *Blade Runner 2049* with the inclusion of characters K and Joi as sentient artificial beings. Consequently, depictions of love involving artificial beings generate doubt as to who is human and who is a machine.

This chapter aims to research Hoffmann's impact on the abovementioned science-fiction narratives. A Freudian approach will be developed to examine the "uncanny" elements in the diverse works. Furthermore, Baudrillard's concepts of "simulacra" and "simulation" will be considered in order to amplify the analysis.

Keywords: Hoffmann, Sandman, Philip K. Dick, Blade Runner, automaton, android, replicant, love, Baudrillard, simulacra

Introduction

German Romantic author E.T.A. Hoffmann (1776-1822) was a major influence on famous writers such as Edgar Allan Poe, Charles Dickens and Charles Baudelaire. Yet the wordsmith and artist also continues to be an inspiration for more modern storytellers. The science-fiction genre may at first glance seem unrelated to the fantasy and Gothic horror author; however, American writer Philip K. Dick (1928-1982) owes a lot to Hoffmann's employment of a female automaton in his story *The Sandman* (1816). This, among other stories, served as incentive for Jacques Offenbach's opera, *The Tales of Hoffmann* (1880), which popularised the plot of the naïve boy who falls in love with a doll. Dick extended this idea in *Do Androids Dream of Electric Sheep?* (1968), blurring the boundaries between humans and androids in a philosophical work. Where at first androids are perceived as a threat, in the end they are presented as feeling the same emotions as individuals, and the lack of empathy some humans possess is disconcerting.

This article will compare the employment of female androids in diverse pieces of fiction: from Hoffmann's automaton and Dick's female cyborgs to the film adaptations *Blade Runner* (1982) and *Blade Runner 2049* (2017). In order to examine the topic, French philosopher Jean Baudrillard's theory of the simulacrum and simulation (1981) will be explained, as well as some brief information about American scholar Donna Haraway and her concept of feminism in relation to cyborgs.

Echoes of Olympia: How Philip K. Dick's female androids resemble Hoffmann's Automaton

Philip K. Dick's *Do Androids Dream of Electric Sheep?* (1968) tells the story of bounty hunter Rick Deckard in a dystopian San Francisco in 1992 (2021 in later editions). His task is to retire six androids which have landed on Earth and represent a threat to the humans they interact with, as they have already murdered several when they fled from Mars. Deckard, who at first carries out his job as regular duty, begins to question his feelings towards the female androids he comes into contact with: Rachael Rosen, who works at the Rosen Association which manufactures the robots, and Luba Luft, one of the cyborgs which escapes to Earth. Consequently, physical attraction is an issue for the married Deckard, whose wife Iran is more focused on the empathy box humans use to share their feelings with other individuals. But how does this plot relate to E.T.A Hoffmann's *The Sandman*? (1816) As this section of the article will analyse, attraction between machines and humans is common to both narratives.

Hoffmann's iconic tale about a young boy, Nathanael, who falls in love with the automaton Olympia has been retold numerous times, and was even the subject of study for Freud in his influential essay *The Uncanny* (1919), though the father of psychoanalysis focused more on the figure of the Sandman himself. To Freud, "He (the Sandman) divides the unfortunate Nathaniel (sic) from his betrothed (Clara) and from her brother, his best friend; he destroys his second object of love, Olympia, the lovely doll; and he drives him into suicide at the moment when he has won back his Clara" (Freud, 1919, p.8). If we consider how Deckard ponders the idea of abandoning his wife and feeling entranced by androids, the similarities begin to emerge.

In *The Sandman*, Nathanael fights with his lover Clara and shouts at her, "You damned lifeless automaton!"; afterwards, Clara remarks, "Oh! he has never loved me, for he does not understand me" (Hoffmann, 1816, p.11). The argument is triggered by Nathanael's attempts to impress his girlfriend with his poetry and taste for the occult, although she is a very rational and methodical person. Nevertheless, Nathanael's accusation is echoed in Dick's novel, as humans behave like machines, while some androids demonstrate empathy.

Dick analysed the thin line between being human and machine, a recurring subject in his fiction. In his speech "The Android and the Human" (1972), he expresses the belief that robots, androids or simulacra, no matter the name they are given, stick to the behaviour their creators develop. He also states that humans think they possess "free will" (p.4) when, in fact, we follow our instincts just as animals do. Therefore, what difference is there between an android, a person and a bee if all of them are ruled by their instincts? This is the main question of *Do Androids Dream of Electric Sheep?*

According to French philosopher Jean Baudrillard, there are three "orders of simulacra": "simulacra that are natural, naturalist… that aim for the restitution or the ideal institution of nature made in God's image"; simulacra that are "a Promethean aim of a continuous globalization and expansion"; and, finally, simulacra "founded on information, the model, the cybernetic game" (Baudrillard, 1981, p.81). Baudrillard considers that the second type of simulacra appears in science fiction, and he mentions how this genre employs values from old "worlds", empties them and reinvents a new society by doing so. Baudrillard even mentions *Simulacra*, by Philip K. Dick (1964) and his use of the War of Secession (Baudrillard, 1994, p.82). In *Do Androids Dream of Electric Sheep?* (1968) the American author creates an apocalyptic world after the so-called World War Terminus, yet there are clear echoes of the American society of the 1960s in his text. Nonetheless, a striking idea in his novel is that androids can develop the same feelings as humans do, and it is in fact the latter who lack emotions.

When Deckard meets Luba Luft at the War Memorial Opera House where she works as a singer of Mozart's *The Magic*

Flute, he is surprised by the quality of her voice, but he also finds the sentiment she needs for her role as Pamina ironic: "However vital, active and nice-looking, an escaped android could hardly tell the truth; about itself, anyhow." (Dick, 1968, p.85)

Surprisingly, artistic features emerge in E.T. A Hoffmann's tale too. Olympia is able to play the piano brilliantly, and sing "as skilfully as an *aria di bravura*" in a voice "almost too brilliant, but clear as glass bells" (Hoffmann, 1816, p.15). Nathanael, incapable of comprehending that Olympia is only a doll, falls deeply in love with her. After the scandal provoked by Nathanael's adoration for the automaton, "several lovers, in order to be fully convinced that they were not paying court to a wooden puppet, required that their mistress should sing and dance a little out of time…but above all things else that she should do something more than listen" (p.20). This results from the fact that Olympia only answers with an "Ah!" and "Goodnight, dear" (p.18). Therefore, the distinctions between women and puppets blur in Hoffmann's story, and men feel threatened by this misunderstanding.

Philip K. Dick's replicants, on the other hand, are powerful in words, and manifest interest in learning about art. Luba Luft is seen staring at a painting by Norwegian artist Edvard Munch: *Puberty*. Deckard even buys her a book about the painter. The choice of painting is paramount, since it exemplifies the experience of Luft herself: an android with the body of a young woman but with childish knowledge of personal relationships. Deckard reflects upon her once she is dead: "But Luba Luft had seemed *genuinely* alive; it had not worn the aspect of a simulation" (Dick, 1968, p.122). As Ian F. Roberts states (2010, p.153), "Luba Luft is very much Olympia's daughter, just as Rick Deckard is a fictional descendant of Hoffmann's

Nathanael". Deckard begins to feel empathy for androids, and he even takes the Voight-Kampff test, which helps distinguish humans from androids, to understand whether his feelings towards them represent a hazard in his profession as a bounty hunter. According to Phil Resch, another bounty hunter who goes so far as to question whether he may be an android himself, "If we included androids in our range of emphatic identification, as we do animals…they'd roll all over us and mash us flat" (Dick, 1968, p.122).

Resch questions his own existence as he has been working together with an android and did not even realise, and his behaviour towards simulacra is rather cruel: "If it's love toward a woman or an android imitation, it's sex. Wake up and face yourself, Deckard. You wanted to go to bed with a female android…Don't kill her – or be present when she's killed – and then feel physically attracted. Do it the other way." (pp.124-125) Therefore, Resch advises Deckard to follow an objectification of androids (as well as of women) and to get rid of them when they become a threat.

When, later on in the novel, Deckard has sex with the android Rachael Rosen, he discovers that she has had sexual intercourse with other bounty hunters in order to stop them from chasing the robots. Moreover, Pris Straton, one of the androids which fled from Mars, resembles Rachael, as the latter points out to Deckard. Therefore, androids are illustrated to be just as manipulative as humans and, when Deckard succeeds in murdering the rest of the androids in one single night, Rachael kills Deckard's goat to punish him, as she is aware of his love for that real animal.

Philip K. Dick had already examined the attraction a human can feel towards an android in his novel *We Can Build You* (1972), a narrative which can be considered a prequel to *Do*

Androids Dream of Electric Sheep? In this story, Louis Rosen falls in love with Pris Frauenzimmer, the schizophrenic daughter of his business partner, who designs the simulacra of Edwin M. Stanton and Abraham Lincoln. Rosen ends up in the mental institution in which Pris is also treated, as he is diagnosed with schizophrenia. There, while being subjected to a treatment involving hallucinogenic drugs, he imagines a life with Pris in which they get married and have children. However, the reality he experiences with Pris is that she is "a woman with eyes of ice, a calculating, ambitious schizoid type, a ward of the Federal Government's Mental Health Bureau who will need psychotherapy the rest of her life… What a woman, what a *thing* to fall in love with. What terrible fate is in store for me now?" (Chapter 12).

Therefore, madness is common to both Dick's and Hoffmann's pieces of fiction. Nathanael screams "Spin round, wooden doll!" (Hoffmann, 1816, p.21) in ecstasy when he sees Coppelius (whom he considers to be the Sandman) at the end of the story. Likewise, Dick's characters dwell in doubt as to whether they are schizoids as they relate with androids.

Yet, how is Hoffman's tale represented in the film adaptation of Dick's story, *Blade Runner*? Is attraction to a simulacrum a risk to humans? Do the androids of the film have feelings? The following section of the article will analyse how emotions are exposed in Ridley Scott's motion picture.

The Eyes of the Sandman in Blade Runner

E.T.A Hoffmann's tale *The Sandman* (1816) contains Northern European folkloric elements, which he uses to create a Gothic story. As a child, Nathanael is told that the Sandman "is a wicked man, who comes to little children when they won't go to bed and throws handfuls of sand in their eyes, so that they jump off their heads all bloody; and he puts them into a bag, and takes them to the half-moon as food for their little ones; and they sit in their nests and have hooked beaks like owls, and they pick naughty little boys' and girls' eyes with them" (p.2).

If we pay close attention to this quote, we can see that the folkloric character is embodied in *Blade Runner*[1] (Scott, 2007). But how is the figure of the Sandman linked to love or the lack of it? This part of the article will examine the connection.

One of the first sequences of Ridley Scott's film depicts a blue eye in which fire is reflected; this is possibly the eye of replicant Roy Batty (Rutger Hauer), the leader of the Nexus-6 androids which Rick Deckard (Harrison Ford) has to hunt. The cyborgs have escaped to Earth, since they wish to make Tyrell Corporation's founder Eldon Tyrell lengthen their four year lifespan. With the slogan "More Human than Human", the company enslaves its replicants in the off-world colonies. The fire reflected in Batty's eye represents the hellish landscape that Earth has become, a setting in which "the angels fall", as Batty states when he misquotes William Blake's *America: A Prophecy* (1793), a book in which the British author condemns slavery. As the plot is developed, the audience witnesses how the replicants, which at first are perceived as the villains, become the chased victims who feel all the emotions humans lack. "Humanity's moral blindness" (Macarthur, 2017, p.383)

1. For this article, the Director's *Final Cut* (2007) version has been used. There were two previous versions of the film, the 1982 original one with Deckard's voice-over narrating the events, and a second version (1992) in which the happy ending was changed, and Deckard's dream sequence was introduced.

is represented by eyes. With the rhyme of "eye" and "I", "the suggestion that the replicants have both, that they can take possession and use 'I' in as full-blooded a sense as anybody else" (Macarthur, 2017, p.384) is portrayed. Philosophy is introduced when Pris (Daryl Hannah), one of the replicants, emphasises "I think, Sebastian, therefore I am" to the designer she and Batty stay with in order to get closer to Tyrell.

Eyes are vital in *Blade Runner*: they distinguish between humans and replicants by the use of the Voight-Kampff test, and, consequently, they illustrate the power humankind has over replicants. In Hoffmann's narrative, Nathanael is convinced that the German lawyer Coppelius is the Sandman himself, and recalls when, as a child, he hid when the appalling man met his father for one of their alchemical experiments. When Coppelius discovers that the child has been listening to them, the lawyer screams: "'Now we've got eyes – eyes – a beautiful pair of children's eyes,' he whispered, and, thrusting his hands into the flames he took out some red-hot grains and was about to throw them into my eyes" (Hoffmann, 1816, p.4). Therefore, burning the eyes and removing them is a threat in the tale. Tyrell does not burn the replicants' eyes, yet does he not employ his emotionally childish creatures to achieve his goals? Does he not create eyes for his androids so that they can be humankind's slaves off-world? The first person visited by replicants Batty and Leon to obtain information is the eye maker Chew. Therefore, eyes are linked to identity as well as to evil, power and slavery.

In the quote mentioned at the beginning of this section, the Sandman is said to have descendants with beaks "like owls". Interestingly, an owl introduces replicant Rachael (Sean Young) in the film, the android with whom detective Deckard falls in love. Eyes are vital in this scene too, as she takes the test to detect whether she is a replicant. However, due to her memory implants, it takes longer to discover she is an android. Eyes here are the embodiment of physical attraction and, as Donna Haraway claims, Rachael "stands as the image of a cyborg culture's fear, love and convulsion" (Haraway, 2016, p.60). For Haraway, a cyborg, a "hybrid of machine and organism" (as such, replicants are cyborgs), is a "matter of fiction and lived experience that changes what counts as women's experiences in the late twentieth century. This is a struggle over life and death, but the boundary between science fiction and social reality is an optical illusion" (Haraway, 1991, p.149). The blurring of the lines between humans and machines, and female androids under the male gaze is exposed in all the above-mentioned pieces of fiction. Beautiful female replicants such as Pris, Zhora (Joanna Cassidy) and Rachael are created to please men, as was Olympia, who "was richly and tastefully dressed. One could not but admire her figure and the regular beauty of her features" (Hoffmann, 1816, p.15). Nevertheless, Nathanael is the only one unaware of the flaws of his beloved: "Yet the striking inward of her back, as well as the wasplike smallness of her waist, appeared to be the result of too-tight lacing…that made an unfavourable impression upon many" (Hoffmann, 1816, p.15).

Nonetheless, Baudrillard emphasises the lack of "doubling" depicted by these cyborgs. In the second version of *Blade Runner* (Scott, 1992), doubts emerge as to whether Deckard is human or a replicant. As detective Gaff (Edward James Olmos) leaves an origami piece in the shape of a unicorn, the same image Deckard daydreams about, the audience remains in doubt about his real nature. Is *Blade Runner* the story of replicants in love? Pris and Roy Batty are enamoured too. These relationships between cyborgs with human feelings are the subject of the

French philosopher's analysis: In *Blade Runner*, "there is no longer a double, one is always already in the other world, which is no longer an other, without a mirror, a projection, or a Utopia that can reflect it – simulation is insuperable, unsurpassable, dull and flat, without exteriority" (Baudrillard, 1981, p.83). Here, the boundaries science fiction had previously created to differentiate humankind from machines become invisible, and the cyborgs dwell unnoticed among individuals.

Like Nathanael, Deckard is, at first, unable to distinguish between the doll/machine and a woman, but his attraction to her does not impede him from seducing her. Had Olympia been able to speak and behave more similarly to a woman, Nathanael would have perhaps started a relationship with her and forgotten Clara. Rachael even plays the piano as Olympia does, and the portrayal of the replicant's feelings occur while she is performing and letting her hair down.

Nevertheless, Rachael is not the only cyborg Deckard has to identify as such: when he arrives at J.F. Sebastian's house, he finds a room full of toys in which Pris disguises herself as a doll with a veil. The confusion between human behaviour and androids continues once Deckard "retires" Pris, as Batty mourns her death and chases the detective.

Roy (meaning "king") Batty ("mad") is the Byronic hero of this film. His poetic soliloquy before dying abounds with religious imagery: he has a white dove in his hand, a nail which echoes Christ's crucifixion, and his words of redemption resemble the coming of the saviour of the replicants: "I've SEEN things you PEOPLE wouldn't believe... All those moments will be lost in time like tears in rain" (emphasis is mine). Nevertheless, the fact that Batty is also a killer emphasises William Blake's influence on the creation of the replicant, as the poet's depiction of Christ in *The Marriage of Heaven and*

Hell (circa 1790) is explained by the Devil himself:

> "…did he not mock at the Sabbath, and so mock the Sabbath's God? Murder those who were murdered because of him? Turn away the law from the woman taken in adultery? Steal the labor of others to support him? Bear false witness when he omitted making a defence before Pilate? Covet when he pray'd for his disciples, and when he bid them shake off the dust of their feet against such as refused to lodge them? I tell you no virtue can exist without breaking these ten commandments. Jesus was all virtue, and acted from impulse, not from rules" (Plate 23)

Replicants are capable of "questionable things", in the same way as Deckard, the hero, murders replicants for a living or humans employ the androids as slaves without any empathy. Nonetheless, once the replicants are eliminated, Deckard can flee with his lover Rachael, although Gaff warns him that, "It's too bad she won't live, but then again who does?". Rachael's lifespan is unknown, yet, as she has been given memories, in my opinion it is likely that she can live longer. Therefore, once the androids are murdered, order seems to be restored. But the ending is unclear: are we seeing two replicants who are in love escaping? Or a man and a replicant?

Interestingly, in Hoffmann's tale, Nathanael dies and order is restored, so that Clara, after some time, can begin a new relationship with another man and be a mother. This traditional role was previously broken when Nathanael rejected her in order to be with a doll. *Blade Runner*'s sequel, *Blade Runner 2049* (2017) transgresses this concept as it is now Rachael, a replicant, who can be a mother. The final section of this article will examine how replicants love and attempt to change the human world they inhabit in Denis Villeneuve's film.

An Automaton Child is Born: The Artistic Replicant in *Blade Runner 2049*

Set thirty years after the original *Blade Runner*, *Blade Runner 2049* (2017) portrays a world in which humans and replicants coexist. A blackout is mentioned several times in the motion picture, an event which is further developed in "a series of three short films produced as side promotional projects for the new film: *Black Out 2022* (Dir. Shinichirō Watanabe, 2017), *2036: Nexus Dawn* (Dir. Luke Scott, 2017), and *2048: Nowhere to Run* (Dr. Luke Scott, 2017)" (Flisfeder, 2017, p.3). These short films explain that when new Nexus 8 models are created after the Nexus 6, they are given a natural lifespan and live among humans. Consequently, humans feel threatened and the so-called "Human Supremacy Movements" use "Tyrell's Replicant records to track down and kill them" (Flisfeder, 2017, p.3). After this, the "Replicant Liberation Movement" destroys all the data centres housing their records, causing the abovementioned blackout that sweeps across the world. The production of replicants is then prohibited, and Tyrell Corporation disappears, but mogul Niander Wallace (Jared Leto) creates new replicants which follow humans' orders, in 2036. In 2049, replicants continue to work for humans, yet they are despised by the individuals they serve.

Blade Runner's sequel begins with Nexus 9 replicant, K (Ryan Gosling), who works for the LAPD (Los Angeles Police Department), chasing and killing Nexus 8 Sapper Morton (Dave Bautista). K's duty is to "retire" all surviving earlier android models, as they threaten the necessary societal order. When he is about to die, Morton declares: "How does it feel, killing your own kind? ...You've never seen a miracle." The miracle he refers to is the birth of Rachael and Deckard's child. Finding the descendant becomes K's task, as lieutenant Joshi (Robin Wright) orders him to find and retire the child, since she believes news of its existence could trigger a war. Her suspicions are correct, as Niander Wallace wishes to find the child to create replicants capable of procreation so that he can use them as slaves in the off-world, while replicants are aiming to start a revolt against humans, with their leader, Freysa Sadeghpour (Hiam Abbass) wishing to murder Deckard. Nevertheless, K suffers a transformation while investigating the case. His priorities shift when he comes to believe that he may be the child, as he suspects his implanted memories may in fact be real.

There is a key novel that can aid in the depiction of K's growth as a character: Vladimir Nabokov's *Pale Fire* (1962), which narrates how a fictional academic, Charles Kinbote, comments on a 999-line poem in four cantos by the also-invented character, John Shade. The verses relate how Shade deals with the suicide of his daughter, among other subjects, and analogies can be made with *Blade Runner 2049*. There are some relevant lines in the first Canto which are echoed in the film, through K, along with Rachael and Deckard's daughter, Ana Stelline (Carla Juri):

> "I was the shadow of the waxwing slain
> By the false azure in the windowpane;
> I was the smudge of ashen fluff – and I
> Lived on, flew on, in the reflected sky…
> Upon that snow, out in that crystal land!
> Retake the falling snow: each drifting flake
> Shapeless and slow, unsteady and opaque,
> A dull dark white against the day's pale white
> And abstract larches in the neutral light."
> (Nabokov, 1962, lines 1-16)

Both K and Stelline live in a cage, K changing his consciousness from the "analytical search for truth to discovering the sensual as truth" (Payne and Pitsis, 2018, p.65), while Ana literally lives in a "bubble", as she suffers from Galatian Syndrome and cannot leave the Earth. They share their journey with one another because K has Ana's memories implanted in his brain. K is like the bird in Nabokov's poem: he cannot see that there is a crystal in his way, so keeps metaphorically crashing against it.

Therefore, Nabokov is crucial to understanding the film; yet, how does this relate to E.T.A. Hoffmann? As has been previously mentioned, Olympia possesses artistic abilities, and she is put on exhibition, playing the piano and singing in front of an audience. Similarly, Ana is an artist, since she literally creates memories for the purpose of alleviating the replicants' hard lives. Where Olympia can create the illusion that she is real and can perform as a human, Ana is the child of a replicant who fabricates fantasies for androids. Furthermore, while Nathanael "remained standing at the window as if glued to the spot by a wizard's spell, his gaze riveted unchangeably upon the divinely beautiful Olympia" (Hoffmann, 1816, p.14), both K and Deckard stare at Ana from outside the bubble in which she works. Both Olympia and Ana are observed through a glass barrier, the former because she lives under the control of her creator, the latter because of a syndrome, which is perhaps faked in order to protect her from being chased.

In the abovementioned examples, snow is employed as a correlation to crystal. In the motion picture, snow links K to Ana: as he (apparently) lies dying beneath falling snowflakes after succeeding in uniting father (Rick Deckard) with daughter (Ana Stelline), a familial beginning is reflected in the virtual snow falling inside Ana's protective bubble as Deckard enters the visiting area.

Nonetheless, these are not the only lines from Nabokov's work employed in the film. Every time K goes on a mission, a special baseline test is presented to him to measure whether he has suffered any emotional deviance. The first time we see K taking the trial in the movie, after killing Morton, he passes:

Interrogator: Recite your baseline.

K: And blood-black nothingness began to spin... A system of cells interlinked within cells interlinked within cells interlinked within one stem... And dreadfully distinct against the dark, a tall white fountain played.

Interrogator: Cells.

K: Cells.

Interrogator: Have you ever been in an institution? Cells.

K: Cells.

Interrogator: Do they keep you in a cell? Cells.

K: Cells.

Interrogator: When you're not performing your duties, do they keep you in a little box? Cells.

K: Cells.

Interrogator: Interlinked.

K: Interlinked.

Interrogator: What's it like to hold the hand of someone you love? Interlinked.

K: Interlinked.

Interrogator: Did they teach you how to feel finger to finger? Interlinked.

K: Interlinked.

Interrogator: Do you long for having your heart interlinked? Interlinked.

K: Interlinked.

Interrogator: Do you dream about being interlinked?

K: Interlinked.

Interrogator: What's it like to hold your child in your arms? Interlinked.

K: Interlinked.

Interrogator: Do you feel that there's a part of you that's missing? Interlinked.

K: Interlinked.

Interrogator: Within cells interlinked.

K: Within cells interlinked.

Interrogator: Why don't you say that three times: Within cells interlinked.

K: Within cells interlinked. Within cells interlinked. Within cells interlinked.

Interrogator: We're done. "Constant K"... you can pick up your bonus.

K: Thank you, sir.

Nevertheless, when K believes that he has actually been birthed, rather than artificially created, and that he may therefore have a soul, he fails the test. The concept of death is emphasised in the line "tall white fountain" (Nabokov, 1962), as this is the image employed by the author in his novel to describe the afterlife, after he suffers a near-death experience. Interestingly, all the questions revolve around being in a cage, physical contact, or the wish to belong in a relationship, and even having a family. This is deeply reflected in K in his relationship with Joi (Ana de Armas), the hologram K buys from Wallace Corporation, and who he keeps as his girlfriend. Joi says she hates *Pale Fire*. She may conceivably detest the narrative because it reflects her existence; she is ostracised in the society of the film, and scorned by replicants as the most inferior of beings.

Nabokov created a protagonist who analysed the work of another fictional character, who can be compared to the humans that created K, Joi's owner. Similar to the original *Blade Runner*, K's partner is dependent on him. With the emanator he buys her, she can move, yet only wherever he goes; she is not a free individual. The female partners of both replicants (if we consider Deckard to be one), belong to them. This male gaze is present when Deckard has a violent sexual encounter with the inexperienced Rachael, and he dominates her; she is attached to him and flees with him, yet the audience never knows what her true feelings for him are. In *Blade Runner 2049*, Joi is the one who gives K a name: Joe. She humanises him and says that she "always knew he was special". Even though she sacrifices herself for him, as at the end of the motion picture she remains in the emanator he buys for her, there is still doubt: Does she really love him? Does she say so because it is her job? When she dies and Joe sees another copy of Joi, he is pensive as he might feel her words are artificial.

Baudrillard considers the hologram to be a "perfect image and end of the imaginary. Or rather, it is no longer an image at all - the real medium is the laser, concentrated light, quintessentialized, which is no longer a visible or reflexive light, but an abstract light of simulation…The double that hid in the depths of you (of your body, of your unconscious?) and whose secret form fed precisely your imaginary" (1981, p.73). Therefore, it can be assumed that Joi utters the words K/Joe wants to hear and behaves as he wants her to. This is precisely Olympia's behaviour with Nathanael. She echoes his wishes and is allegedly the perfect partner for him, although she cannot articulate much vocally. Does K perhaps want to start a family with Joi when he considers himself to be Rachael and

Deckard's child? The film does not reveal this, yet the viewer is made aware of his real love for her and his need for affection.

K's actions are the result of love in the same way as Roy Batty's were in the original *Blade Runner*. While K concentrates on uniting a miraculous daughter with her father, Batty emerges as a saviour-like figure who absolves Deckard's life and, consequently, his sins. Both replicants, old and new, are "more human than human", since they demonstrate more empathy and kindness than the individuals present in both pieces of fiction. Besides, the poetic aspect both replicants share unfolds a number of philosophical questions, which is why K's (apparent) death in the snow pays homage to Batty's. The ending of the film, with the reunion of Deckard and Ana, echoes this concept of the love replicants yearn for, with the hope of a positive future within their family.

Conclusion

Modern society's increasing use of robots and cyborgs has long been a trope in science fiction. The fact that machines can rebel against their human creators is also a common feature in this kind of narrative. However, machines are not always given feelings when living in our society. This shifting of roles in which replicants/androids express more feelings than humans, and even develop romantic relationships, is a key characteristic in Philip K. Dick's *Do Androids Dream of Electric Sheep?* Nevertheless, the concept of falling in love with a machine was already developed by German author E.T.A. Hoffmann in his tale *The Sandman*.

This article has compared Hoffmann's automaton with Dick's androids, both in his written narratives and in *Blade Runner*, the film adaptation of his novel, and its sequel, *Blade*

Runner 2049. More than two hundred years after Hoffmann wrote his story, we are still wondering whether it is possible to have feelings for an artificial being, be it an automaton, a replicant, or a hologram. Yet the future will probably give us a wider variety of artificial beings to fall in love with and huge narratives to develop these relationships, once more blurring the boundaries between human and machine.

Bibliography

Baudrillard, J., 1981. *Simulacra and Simulation*, [pdf] Available at: <https://www.e-reading.club/bookreader.php/144970/Baudrillard_-_Simulacra_and_Simulation.pdf> [Accessed 10 September 2019]

Blade Runner, 1982. [film] Ridley Scott. USA: The Ladd Company, Shaw Brothers, Blade Runner Partnership.

Blade Runner - The Director's Cut, 1992. [film] Ridley Scott. USA: Warner Bros.

Blade Runner - The Final Cut, 2007. [film] Ridley Scott. USA: Warner Bros.

Blade Runner 2049, 2017. [film] Denis Villeneuve. USA: Alcon Entertainment, Columbia Pictures, Bud Yorkin Productions, Torridon Films, 16:14 Entertainment, Thunderbird Entertainment, Scott Free Productions.

Blake, W., 1793. *America: A Prophecy*. Available at: <https://archive.org/details/americaprophecy00blakuoft/page/1> [Accessed 15 September 2019]

---, circa 1793. *The Marriage of Heaven and Hell*. Available at: <http://www.blakearchive.org/copy/mhh.h?descId=mhh.h.illbk.23> [Accessed 15 September 2019]

Dick, K.P., 1964. *The Simulacra*. New York: Ace Books.

---, 1968, *Do Androids Dream of Electric Sheep?* London: Orion Publishing Group.

---, 1972. *The Android and the Human* [pdf] Available at: <https://sporastudios.org/mark/courses/articles/Dick_the_android.pdf> [Accessed 3 October 2019]

---, 1972. *We Can Build You.* [Kindle Version] Available at: <http://www.amazon.es> [Accessed 30 September 2019]

Flisfeder, M., 2017. Beyond Heaven and Hell: This World is All We've Got: *Blade Runner 2049* in Perspective. *Red Wedge Magazine*, [online] Available at: <www.redwedgemagazine.com/online-issue/beyond-heaven-and-hell-this-world-is-all-weve-got-blade-runner-2049-in-perspective?utm_campaign=shareaholic&utm_medium=printfriendly&utm_source=tool>

[Accessed 20th November 2019]

Freud, S., 1919. *The Uncanny* [pdf] Available at: <http://web.mit.edu/allanmc/www/freud1.pdf> [Accessed 30 August 2019]

Haraway, D., 2016. *A Cyborg Manifesto: Science, Technology, and Socialist-Feminism in the Late Twentieth Century*, [online] Available at: <https://warwick.ac.uk/fac/arts/english/currentstudents/undergraduate/modules/fictionnownarrativemediaandtheoryinthe21stcentury/manifestly_haraway_-----a_cyborg_manifesto_science_technology_and_socialist-feminism_in_the_....pdf> [Accessed 2 September 2019]

---, 1991. *Simians, Cyborgs and Women: The Reinvention of Nature*, [online] Available at: <https://monoskop. org/images/f/f3/Haraway_Donna_J_Simians_Cyborgs_and_Women_The_Reinvention_of_Nature.pdf> [Accessed 20 September 2019]

Hoffmann, E.T.A., 1816. *The Sandman* [pdf] Available at: <http://art3idea.psu.edu/metalepsis/texts/sandman.pdf> [Accessed 15 September 2019]

Macarthur, D., 2017. A Vision of Blindness: *Blade Runner* and Moral Redemption. *Film-Philosophy*, [e-journal] 21(3), pp.371-391. Available at: <https://www.euppublishing.com/doi/pdfplus/10.3366/film.2017.0056> [Accessed 20 December 2017]

Nabokov, V., 1962. *Pale Fire* [pdf] Available at: <http://www.24grammata.com/wp-content/uploads/2011/12/Nabokov-Pale-Fire-24grammata.com_.pdf> [Accessed 20 September 2019]

Payne, C. and Pitsis, A., 2018. On Nature and the Tactility of the Senses in *Blade Runner 2049*. *Journal of Asia-Pacific Pop Culture*, [e-journal] 3(1), pp.55-74. Available at: <https://www.jstor.org/stable/pdf/10.5325/jasiapacipopcult.3.1.0055.pdf?refreqid=excelsior%3A150a244ee153a919ed1fdf22253d51af> [Accessed 20 October 2019]

Roberts, I. R, 2010. Olympia's Daughters: E.T.A. Hoffmann and Philip K. Dick. *Science Fiction Studies*, [e-journal] 37 (1), pp.150-153. Available through: JSTOR <https://www.jstor.org/stable/40649606?readnow=1&seq=4#page_scan_tab_contents> [Accessed 30 September 2019]

Banners and baby factories: the romantic cost of better breeding

Christina Lake

Abstract

What happens when love becomes subservient to state policy? Does control over reproductive freedom necessarily involve a negative impact on the right to love? And is there ever a sufficiently compelling reason to regulate who is allowed to have children? I explore these questions through a comparison of two satirical dystopian works written in the inter-war years, Rose Macaulay's *What Not* and Aldous Huxley's *Brave New World*, set against two recent works of science fiction that share some of the same concerns, Carrie Vaughn's *Bannerless* and Anne Charnock's *Dreams Before the Start of Time*. Whereas the earlier works reflect and satirise the early twentieth century's obsession with eugenics and measuring intelligence, the later works focus more on fears of overpopulation and the dehumanising effects of rapidly developing reproductive technologies. However, in all four works love becomes a way of assessing the emotional impact of the changes explored, and offers a focus for resistance to ideas of rational reproduction. There are also strong links between the works in terms of their ambivalence over the benefits of controlling reproduction, the importance of personal choice and fears of where rapid changes to technology might lead. I argue that in all of these, love is represented as a disruptive element, stronger than scientific hopes for a more sustainable way of planning for future generations.

*

In the late nineteenth century, Victorian polymath Francis Galton came up with the idea that the world could be improved by encouraging the best people to marry each other. He coined the term eugenics and created a controversial pseudoscience around the idea of improving humans through eliminating those deemed hereditarily unfit and offering incentives for the so-called right people to have more children. Galton (1908) hoped to turn eugenics into a mass popular movement, with local eugenics societies up and down the country, and towards the end of his life, wrote a work of utopian fiction, 'Kantsaywhere', featuring a society where marriage was regulated by eugenic exams (Galton and Sargant, 2001). Richardson (2003, p.85) argues that "At the core of 'Kantsaywhere' lies a new, rationalized love; passion—an inhibitor of rational choice—was edited out of the love plot". Instead women were supposed to consider their duty to the next generation when choosing husbands, and indeed many feminists were attracted to eugenics by "a promise of a new morality" and a role in the "'rational control' of the nation's reproduction" (Bland, 2001, pp.229-30). However, Rose Macaulay took issue with this idea of rational reproduction in *What Not: A Prophetic Comedy* (1918), a satirical dystopian novel where there are rewards and punishments for couples according to how desirable it is for them to have children, and love is ruthlessly set aside for marriages based on intelligence. But the idea of rational reproduction still persists in the present day. For example, Carrie Vaughn's *Bannerless* (2017) also looks at rationalising reproduction, but for population control rather than population improvement. In her post-apocalyptic society, households have to earn banners that give them the right to have a child.

While the technological level of Vaughn's society requires women to remain responsible for contraception, ectogenesis or the artificial womb, as mooted by J. B. S. Haldane in 'Daedalus; or science and the Future' (1924) offered another route to rationalising production of improved human beings and taking love out of the equation. Aldous Huxley ran with the idea in *Brave New World* (1932), where babies emerge from a production line, already categorised and genetically modified to fit their role in life, and love is replaced by unlimited sexual freedom and mind-numbing drugs. Haldane and Huxley's visions have persisted into the twenty-first century where in vitro fertilisation, cloning and other medical techniques combine with gene editing to revive questions of genetically engineering the perfect child. Anne Charnock's *Dreams Before the Start of Time* (2017) picks up on Huxley's scientifically managed baby factories to investigate the implications for love, family and relationships of the possible trajectory of this technology.

Critics have argued that "[f]alling in love (Gottlieb, 2001, p.21) or "illicit sexual arousal" (Horan, 2007, p.315) are important sources of political awakening and resistance to a dystopian regime. In this article I examine whether this argument holds true for *What Not* and *Brave New World*, given the ambivalence in these texts over the consequences of love and its representation as a barrier to scientific progress. I will then explore whether love can still have the same subversive potential in twenty-first century science fiction in an age of freely available contraception, sexual diversity and less restrictive social mores. I will look at how love affects projects for controlling and genetically engineering reproduction in the Bannerless saga and *Dreams Before the Start of Time*, and argue that there remain elements of love that continue to resist rational control.

Rose Macaulay's *What Not* was written towards the end

of the First World War, and set in a projected near future where a bureaucratic government has taken on the task of preventing future wars by attempting to raise the general level of intelligence of the population. In this barely alternative post-war London, there are commuter air buses with an alarming tendency to crash land, a "Ministry of Brains" and a "Directorate of Entertainments", not to mention The Hidden Hand, the daily governmental newspaper that takes care of propaganda. Despite these dystopian sounding organs, the atmosphere of the book is satirical not oppressive. The chief innovation is the policy of categorising the entire population by level of intelligence, and then devising complicated rules as to who might marry whom: "If you were classified A, your brains were certified to be of the highest order, and you were recommended to take a B2 or B3 partner (these were quite intelligent)". Meanwhile those classified as C were discouraged from having children, by fines and ultimately imprisonment if they should have more than three children (Macaulay, 2019, p.15). Macaulay is clearly making fun of the kind of schemes proposed by eugenicists. For example, Galton (1865, p.319) suggested dividing the population into two groups, A, the naturally talented and B "the refuse" and introducing measures "that would somewhat hasten the marriages in caste A, and retard those in caste B" resulting in "a larger proportion of children being born to A than to B" with the aim of "wholly eliminating B, and replacing it by A".

Later eugenicists proposed such schemes as bonuses, tax breaks and educational benefits for children from desirable parents. "The need for encouraging early marriage and parenthood among the efficient cannot be too strongly advocated" wrote Sybil Gotto (1917, p.185), founder of the Eugenics Education Society, while in an essay from 1914 H. G. Wells (2013, p.76) suggested an early version of family allowances to be paid to mothers "dependent on the quality of the home in which the children are being reared, upon their health and physical development, and upon their educational success".

Concerns over intelligence, or its reverse, the proliferation of the so-called feeble-minded, were also high in the public consciousness. The Mental Deficiency Act of 1913, which legalised the confinement to institutions of those deemed mentally subnormal, was passed with very little opposition, although a previous version of the act that recommended sterilisation was opposed (Gilbert). In Macaulay's England there is instead a Mental Progress Act (2019, p.15), which as well as regulating marriages based on intelligence, also refused certification to those with a hereditary deficiency in their family. This possibility of being highly intelligent but uncertificated for marriage becomes a key plot point in Macaulay's novel, and allows the consequences of restrictions on marriage to be viewed not solely from the disempowered and unvoiced perspective of those deemed feeble-minded, as so often occurred in debates on the subject, but from that of articulate central protagonists.

Macaulay's satire picks up on these currents of eugenics and fear of mental disability, but injects a more human element into them, firstly by imagining how such measures would go down with the war-weary British public and secondly by exploring the effects of love on the scientific logic of the programme. Macaulay divides her narrative perspective between two characters working for the Ministry of Brains: Ivy Delmer, a young innocent, the daughter of a Vicar and the rakish and more worldly-wise Kitty Grammont. Ivy's role is to demonstrate the gap between the policy of the Ministry and its effects on ordinary people, such as her father's parishioners in the imaginary Buckinghamshire village of Little Chantreys. She comes to realise that all the abstract rules and regulations of the Ministry actually affect people she knew, for example, families with over three children and "the courting boys and girls on stiles in Buckinghamshire lanes" (Macaulay, 2019, p.19). The most comedic episodes play out in Little Chantreys, a village where, as the playful voice of the narrator suggests, the mice are more intelligent than the people (p.47). Brains Sunday and the launch of the Government Mind Training Course is not a success there. The Vicar preaches against the "Directorate of Matrimony" and questions whether there is scriptural backing for the idea of only marrying the clever (p.53). A baby show where the merits of a well-bred baby are compared to those of an uncertificated baby ends in shambles when in turns out that the wrong baby is being held up as a model of intelligent breeding. Unintended consequences abound with babies being left on doorsteps to escape fines. Eventually Ivy, disenchanted, plans to leave the Ministry to go against the regulations herself and marry someone classified as less intelligent than her:

I'm B3 and he's C1 (though I'm certain they've classified him wrong, because he's not a bit stupid really …), but of course it's against the regulations for us to marry each other.

Although she is meant to marry someone more intelligent than herself, Ivy cannot imagine an "A person" loving her in the same way (p.157). Marrying according to some schema drawn up by government ministers is simply not realistic for those wanting compatible partners, and marrying upward for Ivy would mean class differences as well as different belief systems and morality.

Ivy's courtship by the C1 man is not dramatized, but a

different love affair between Kitty Grammont and the Minister of Brain, Nicky Chester, is, adding a serious element to Macaulay's free-ranging satire on the Ministry, the press and the state of intelligence of the ordinary man (and woman) on the London Underground. Kitty and Nicky's affair is not just an inappropriate workplace romance, but a scandal under the new regulations, as Nicky Chester is not certified to marry due to mental deficiency in his family.

What is at stake when the two give in to their love and get married is the very survival of the regime, and everything that Nicky Chester believes in. Lonsdale in her introduction to the new edition of *What Not* sees this decision as the chief problem of the novel. By having Chester making such a selfish and hypocritical decision, without "a flicker of introspection", she argues that Macaulay puts "part of the novel's structure in jeopardy" (Lonsdale, 2019, p.xxii). At the time of writing the novel, Macaulay had started a secret relationship with a married man, and there is no doubt that some of her own feelings of guilt and passion influence how she represents the affair, but ultimately the part that love plays is crucial to the argument of the novel. Aside from Macaulay's obvious amusement at seeing her two supposedly intelligent A-grade protagonists caught in a quandary "straight out of a comic opera" (Macaulay, 2019, p.106), she suggests love is part of what makes people stupid.

Nicky Chester's crusade to make people more intelligent comes from his personal experience of mental disability in his family. He grew up "loathing stupidity in the way that some few people (conceivably) loathe vice" (p.148) and from there came to hate stupidity in general as the biggest barrier to improving the world. Nicky's experiment in practical eugenics is a personal and emotional one, a drive to make people see stupidity "for the limp, hopeless, helpless animal thing it is – an idiot drivelling on a green" (p.74). Kitty realises that by falling in love, Nicky has been caught in the "destroying grip" of that same beast he is out to defeat, because it makes him just as stupid as anybody else (Macaulay, 2019, p.131). Kitty herself sees love as a "queer disease" at odds with "principle, chivalry, common sense, intellect, humour, culture, sweetness and light, all we call civilisation" and one of the main obstacles to humans becoming "a clever and successful race" (p.130). This somewhat depressing conclusion suggests that Macaulay was well aware of the potentially destructive power of love.

While sexual desire is seen in this negative light as an impediment to human progress, Macaulay makes it clear that the Ministry's plans never had much of a chance in the first place. At the end of the day, it is not the hypocrisy of Nicky Chester that brings it down, but people's general unwillingness to accept coercion in matters of the human heart. Macaulay observes that even though people could become accustomed to all kinds of infringements on their freedom, such as: "Education, vaccination, taxation, sanitation, representation", a Ministry that "deliberately and coldly stood between lover and lover" (pp.170, 168) was never going to succeed. Love does not radicalise the protagonists, but it does promote passive resistance. Ultimately, Chester's own love affair teaches him the lesson that "People were determined not to stand laws that inconvenienced them" (p.180). This conclusion shows that Macaulay does not see Galton-style eugenic schemes as a viable route to human progress, because in questions of love and marriage, individual desire tends to win out over social responsibility. Emery (1991, p.177), one of Macaulay's biographers, sums it up well:

> *What Not* offers the bemused sense of a muddled world: the
> author-narrator is for a more intelligent citizenry but against
> any legal coercion that would create it; the writer's fictional
> voice celebrates the joy of romantic love but laments its
> inevitable destructive selfishness.

In *Brave New World*, Aldous Huxley deals with this issue
of human resistance to being improved by setting up a factory
system for producing babies to order. Stealing liberally from
his friend Haldane's idea of ectogenesis, and possibly, it has
been speculated, from Macaulay for his classification system,
the babies are produced to order in alarmingly large batches
of identical siblings, ready categorised by intelligence from
alpha through to epsilon. All in the name of social stability
and efficiency. Every child is genetically engineered and
conditioned to fit its place in society. The rules are less complex
than in Macaulay's satire. People only associate with those of
their own class and hypnopaedia and aversion therapy are used
to reinforce this rigid social hierarchy. While these divisions
are required for keeping society stable, there are no heredity
consequences to liaisons between classes, as humans are no
longer "viviparous", that is natural childbirth no longer occurs.
Viviparous reproduction is seen as primitive and physically
repugnant, and "mother" is a rude word unless used in a medical
context. Only 30% of women are even capable of pregnancy,
a facility retained to maintain biodiversity should anything go
wrong with the factory system.

People lack freedom, but they have a hedonistic lifestyle of
freely available sex and drugs to deliver the illusion of happiness.
Huxley's theory was that "As political and economic freedom
diminishes, sexual freedom tends compensatingly to increase"
(2004, p.xlix). He also thought that the reverse was true, and that

social energy could come from sexual continence, as theorised by anthropologist J. D. Unwin (1940), who proposed that to maintain an ideal society people (meaning men) should be able to choose between an alpha marriage of strict monogamy with access to high social and political positions, or a beta marriage of easy dissolution in favour of sensual satisfaction. Huxley (1940, p.18) saw the choice starkly as between sensuality and power, concluding that: "The social mechanism proposed by Unwin would make it possible for people to lose the world for love or love for the world with the minimum friction and discomfort and the maximum awareness of the consequences of choice". The fact that Huxley did not perceive monogamous marriage as a likely outcome for those of a sensual disposition is a telling indication of his attitudes to love. In an essay on 'Fashions in Love', Huxley (1929, p.135) criticised restrictive romantic concepts of love as instruments of "social utility" and no more "divine" or "natural" than any other form of love. Birnbaum (1966, pp.291-292) justly summarises Huxley's representation of love in his novels as "a choice between the enslavement with a passion largely imagined and the debauchery and self-abasement which are the consequences of passionless love".

In *Brave New World* romantic love is taboo. Mustapha Mond, one of ten controllers of the World State, reverses the usual critiques of sexual infidelity to blame monogamy, romance and family life for the psychological problems that destabilise the world (Huxley, 2004, p.34). Intercut with this, embryo technician Lenina has to defend herself from the criticism of having sexual relations with the same person for four months in a row, and not being "a little more promiscuous" (2004, p.36). The mantra "Everyone belongs to everyone else" is repeated to outlaw exclusive relationships and therefore the psychological damage of thwarted desire. But in the process women are objectified and conditioned to respond to the requirement to be sexually available to as many men as possible. Although this is a theoretically equal arrangement, the conversations of the women suggest a desire to get away from this duty through monogamy or fake pregnancy, while the men continue to boast about how often they have "had" different women.

Huxley does set up a counterpoint to this attitude through the perspective of Bernard Marx, the substandard Alpha who resents the casual way his fellow alpha males refer to Lenina: "Have her here, have her there. Like mutton. Degrading her to so much mutton" (2004, p.39). At first it looks like Huxley is setting up a narrative where love between Marx and Lenina will triumph over the conditioning of society and unravel the illusion of happiness to move to a truer state of happiness. In setting out Marx's failure to bond with his solidarity group, we are shown a character who does not buy in to the mores of his society. He is immune to conditioning, either through some flaw in the production process as an embryo, or because he is a hypnopedia expert in charge of conditioning others. He dislikes the slogans and platitudes that others such as Lenina are always expressing, and seeks out more authentic experiences. But in doing so, Marx falls back onto romantic tropes of wanting to spend time with Lenina looking at sunsets or gazing out across the ocean, activities that mean nothing to Lenina, who has been conditioned to value her self-worth in gifts and the sexual satisfaction of her partner. Ultimately, Marx is an unsatisfactory representative of romantic love, a bitter, socially maladjusted personality, quick to perceive imaginary slights whose love for Lenina can be seen as simply another symptom of his maladjustment. In any case, the role of misguided romantic lead is taken over by another character partway through the novel: John the Savage, the natural man born through a failure of contraceptives to a beta woman accidentally stranded on an Indian Reservation in New Mexico. John's values and language are derived from a battered volume of the works of Shakespeare, so it is no surprise that he too falls in love with Lenina. But his concept of love involves women being pure and flawless, and does not accommodate Lenina's cheerful promiscuity. It is not her he loves, but an idea of her, and he is "terrified lest she should cease to be something he could feel himself unworthy of" (Huxley, 2004, p.147). Whilst not a fully-realised character, Lenina is slightly more than a passive love object. Although only seen in short vignettes, Lenina clearly has a wistful need for love, even if she only knows how to enact it through sex. In her earliest appearance, she is trying to break an addiction to only dating one man, then she takes a risk on Bernard Marx, despite his unpopularity, and finally experiences all the symptoms of love in relation to John the Savage, discovering that "Love is as good as soma" or like the beginnings of a "Violent Passion Surrogate treatment" (Huxley, 2004, pp.145,152). Love here is positioned as another drug, but what is interesting is that this passion proves to be stronger than Lenina's conditioning, and as Gottlieb (2001, p.71) argues turns her too into a subversive.

With Macaulay, it is clear that however much it might be desirable to improve humans, innate human instincts, such as love, would prevent it. Huxley's society bypasses resistance through manipulating these instincts, producing empty jaded people incapable of forming real relationships. While Huxley represents romantic love as another form of conditioning, he also admits its disruptive potential and capacity to make people feel more deeply, but also make them less happy. The closing arguments between John the Savage and Mustapha Mond, the

World Controller, poses the question of whether it is better to have a stable world where most of the people are happy most of the time, or a passionate world full of creativity and life but also neuroses, sickness, war and painful death. It is unclear who wins the argument. The technological changes of *Brave New World* were developed in response to a destructive war, and its aims, if not its methods, seem to be endorsed by Huxley. However, in his utopian novel *Island* (1962), Huxley recognises the potential of love to create social cohesion, and develops a religion of love which offers both stability and meaningful relationships. In this respect, love becomes a third alternative to the options developed in *Brave New World*, but also one of the techniques for preventing dissent and achieving new goals such as population control. By the late 1950s "the problem of rapidly increasing numbers in relation to natural resources, to social stability and to the well-being of individuals" had become a central issue for Huxley (1974, pp.17-18).

Some 60 years later, Carrie Vaughn's *Bannerless* series shares the same concern about keeping population levels in balance with natural resources. The post-apocalyptic Coast Road communities of the series enforce mandatory birth control to restrict population growth, and the right to have a child has to be earned, to ensure that "every baby born will be provided for, will have a place, and won't overburden what we have" (Vaughn, 2016b, p.281). Vaughn explores this world through a number of stories including the Hugo-nominated 'Amaryllis' (2010) and the short story 'Bannerless' (2015), which introduced the character of Enid, the Investigator who is the chief protagonist of the two novels written so far, *Bannerless* (2017) and *The Wild Dead* (2018). The novels have been well received for their kindness, hopefulness and community values in a genre which usually presents grim and violent post-apocalyptic scenarios (Robertson, 2017 and Bourke, 2018). Vaughn's interest is in the rebuilding of civilisation and the realities of establishing communities, the need for mutual support and, through the character of Enid, the need for someone to enforce rules. For Vaughn "the libertarian ideal of individuals working cooperatively" has to be set "against the reality that there always seems to be that one person screwing it up for everyone else, hence the need for some kind of governance" (Coleman, 2017). By focusing on individuals, those who live by the rules, those who enforce them and those who disobey, Vaughn humanises what would otherwise seem like an extreme example of government interference. In her world, there is no longer any automatic right to have children. Only those who have proved that they can provide for a child, a status acknowledged through the awarding of a banner, are allowed to breed. Some communities can simply never earn banners, because they do not have the resources to support children. All girls are given contraceptive implants at puberty, and there are stiff penalties for anyone found to have removed their implant.

Macaulay's post-WW1 society did not tolerate government interference in the right to procreate, but Vaughn's Coast Road communities by and large accept it. One reason for their complicity in this arrangement is that they can still partner up with whoever they like; there is widespread sexual freedom, as well as acceptance of homosexuality and diversity. As in *Brave New World*, the restrictions are a trade-off for security. Vaughn (2018) explains:

> There's an aspect of protection to it – people are part of this society because it's safe. …. Even with all the restrictions, it's a good place to be. People agree to the rules in exchange for that safety.

But it remains striking that banners, and the associated children, have become the chief element of the reward and punishment system of the Coast Road. Individuals work to earn a banner. Punishments involve banning households from ever having banners. Crimes are often committed for banners. And a whole new apparatus of investigation has been set up to regulate the process. The system of quotas and punishments is reminiscent of the situation in China, where the one-child policy of population control has led to families being impoverished for infringements and babies being hidden or forcibly taken for adoption (Johnson, 2016). For example, the short story 'Bannerless' sees Enid and her partner Bert following a tip-off about an unauthorised pregnancy. Their power to break up households and inflict punishment on mother and child evidently makes everyone very nervous around them. One character even believes that they might "rip the baby out, cut its throat, leave us to bleed to death as a warning" (Vaughn, 2016b, pp.275-276). While no such atrocities take place in Vaughn's Coast Road communities, we learn that a bannerless baby is likely to be removed from its parents and given to a new family to avoid the child being blamed for the circumstances of its birth. Bannerless children "grow up thinking they have to work twice as hard to earn their place in the world" (Vaughn, 2016b, p.281), or like Marie in 'Amaryllis', who was born without a banner, wonder if they were worth the price her mother paid for their existence (Vaughn, 2016a, p.290).

The mixture of emotions and passions that lead to banner infringements are set against the grounded values of Enid. The novel *Bannerless* explores these values through Enid's life story and in particular through different concepts of love. In the back story, Enid falls passionately in love with Dak, an itinerant guitar player, and learns about herself through travelling with him and experiencing his casual approach to love. In the "present day" timeline of the book, Enid investigates a crime motivated by a jealous and a more possessive type of love, the sort that she hoped had been left behind in the old world:

> All that, for a bit of jealousy and misguided anger. Jealousy was a nebulous thing until you were the one feeling it …. But they were supposed to be *better* than that. Better than the old world. (Vaughn 2017, p.272)

Enid meets up with Dak again, but this time she is not taken in by his "gentle, wheedling, bardic charm" (p. 269), preferring the more supportive love of her partner Sam and her household with its common room "full of love and safety" (2016b, p.284). What is being proposed is a more responsible love, one that will accept that banners and babies have to be earned, and that having a child is a "privilege not a right" (2017, p.54). Even Dak, the ultimate wanderer, wants to settle down and earn a banner. Like the eugenic feminists of the late nineteenth century, *Bannerless* attempts to redefine love and remove passion from the equation. It is this redefined love, akin to kindness, which dominates the tone of the stories and prevents them from reading as dystopias. Instead there is a pragmatic idealism about their aims: "They wanted a world that would let them survive not just longer but better. They aimed for utopia knowing they'd fall short…" (2016b, p.289)

However, the banner system, while kind, still excludes those members of society who cannot or will not work for banners. It is as eugenically efficient as anything dreamt up by Francis Galton. The best members of society, defined as those who are the most honest, hard-working and liked by their community, will get the banners. And those with more antisocial personality traits, who do not wish to live in the extended families of the successful banner earners, will be bred out of existence. There is even a bit of genetic enhancement going on. Women can choose who they like to father a child, from beyond their household, such as Tomas, Enid's mentor, or Dak, whose good looks and musical ability might make him an attractive proposition. At least there is no evidence of cultural bias towards male children, and the issue of disability is handled sensitively through the representation of a young man with Down's syndrome who is loved and cared for by his community.

The bannerless system avoids the pitfalls of controlled breeding represented in *What Not*'s satire on eugenic schemes. But despite the greater buy-in to the scheme, it still needs regulating and still gets gamified or disregarded. Love and other human passions are not as biddable as Enid would like to hope. In *Dreams Before the Start of Time*, Anne Charnock (2017) explores what the free market in genetic enhancement might look like, and whether love can survive the advent of options to reproduce without a partner. This book, which won the Arthur C. Clarke award in 2018, consists of a series of connected stories representing several generations of families over a time period of 86 years up to 2120. While in *Brave New World* all children are gestated in artificial wombs, Charnock's novel follows the transition from natural childbirth being the norm to a two-tier system where those who can afford it have genetically enhanced children through remote gestation. Love is one of the lenses through which the book examines issues such as artificial donor insemination, solo parenting and gene editing. While romantic/sexual relationships are no longer necessary for having children, there's a sense of yearning for love and the perfect match. At the same time, new technologies seem to be undermining love. Millie's decision to get donor sperm for her pregnancy causes a rift with her on-off boyfriend. The option for commitment-free co-parenting almost causes Toni to abort her naturally conceived baby in favour of cleaned up sperm and "a special FOREVER friend", which after breaking up with her previous long-term boyfriend seems to her a more realistic prospect than finding a "forever boyfriend" (Charnock, 2017, p.23). Both Millie and Toni consider non-traditional routes to parentage, as they have lost faith in the dating system as a means of securing a long-term partner. Millie identifies as asexual, but still feels let down when her boyfriend goes off travelling, and so opts to co-parent with her gender fluid sister. There is a sense of the new reproductive technology developing in response to the changing societal mores around relationships.

In the next generation, Millie's son Rudy and his girlfriend Simone consider adopting an orphan foetus gestating remotely in a baby clinic, a facility which with its lines of foetuses in glass bottles evokes the baby factories of *Brave New World* while also making adopting a child seem more like buying a puppy. When the adoption does not work out, Rudy and Simone opt for a new technology which would allow them to have a child based solely on Rudy's own genetic material, as Simone refuses to have a child biologically related to herself due to bad experiences with her own family. This level of genetic choice offers a tailor-made family, but leads closet romantic Dr. Kristina Christophe, who performs the genetic manipulation, to see this decision as "So many shades of fucked up" (p.95), as Rudy and Simone could easily have had their own child without assistance. This verdict seems to encapsulate the relationships brought about by the new technology. Rudy goes along with Simone's wishes out of love, as his experiences of his mother and aunt's chaotic love life leaves him determined to have a committed long-term monogamous relationship himself (Charnock, 2017, p.81). The new options, which in Huxley's view would dismantle the family and sidestep neuroses, in Charnock's stories just seem to make these neuroses worse. A whole set of new complexes arise, whether an obsession with the perfect mother from a solo conceived child, risks of accidentally having a relationship with a fellow descendant of a prolific sperm donor or problems with a genetically enhanced child fitting into the existing family.

The novel has been criticised for its "ableist prejudices" and for "never truly question[ing] its own basic premise of 'fixing' people" (Nadkarni, 2018). Although the novel shows genetic enhancement as a mixed benefit, with the unenhanced children represented as being more creative and outgoing than the enhanced children, it does not take on board the ethical questions surrounding editing out disability, leaving it open to the charge of supporting eugenics. Disability activists rightly point out that if certain conditions, such as autism or Down's syndrome, are seen as abnormal traits to be eliminated from the human genome, then the lives of those with these conditions will be devalued and the definition of what constitutes a human will become limited (Garland-Thomson, 2012). While not tackling these issues, Charnock does cover a wide-ranging set of genetic possibilities and explores the consequences of the new liberal eugenics, described by ethicist Michael J Sandel as "a way for privileged parents to have the kind of children they want and to arm them for success in a competitive society." (2009, p.78). Sandel criticises genetic enhancement for undermining humility and solidarity and placing a moral responsibility on parents to provide as much genetic enhancement as possible for their children (2009, p.86). Charnock represents these issues from a variety of perspectives, at the level of individuals caught up in trying to understand the new scientific options and make good decisions for themselves and their children. In doing so, she demonstrates the emotional factors that go into such decisions, regardless of how rational they might sound, and the difficulty of foreseeing the consequences.

The complexity of the issues around human enhancement – from wanting to improve the intelligence of the population through to genetic engineering – show the importance of representations of emotion such as love that move the debates from the abstract into the human reality. It is no coincidence that love as a human emotion is one of the key elements for testing how such social or technological changes might affect individuals. Romantic love is particularly crucial to the question of reproductive enhancement, as for the past century it has been the chief means of determining sexual relationships that result in children. The downgrading of romantic love in favour of a more utilitarian approach to choosing partners and co-parents has not been without emotional consequences. The idea of rational reproduction continues to be at odds with the concepts of love, desire, mutual support and human freedom. Each of the novels I examine here show what would be lost if reproduction for the good of society were privileged over individual desire. While it could be argued that in some cases the societal benefits of the projects for change might outweigh the individual harm to greater or lesser degrees, the novels demonstrate that the ability to love freely is an important factor in the success or failure of projected changes. For Macaulay, the human desire for sexual love prevents the proposed system of eugenic marriages ever being successful, while for Huxley love reveals the vacuous meaninglessness and lack of depth to life in his *Brave New World*. However, for the twenty-first century writers, the role of love and romantic relationships has become uncertain when decoupled from reproduction. In Vaughn's *Bannerless* stories, love needs to be responsible and mature, not self-centred or jealous, but remains one of the factors that cannot totally be controlled by the banner police. For Charnock, the new possibilities opened up by genetic technologies and remote gestation offer the opportunity to dispense with the traditional models of loving relationships, but her characters discover that the need for love and stability remain as strong as ever. In the end, love acts as an important emotional reality check on attempts at turning reproduction into an industry, or regulating when and how people might be allowed to have children. However, the kind of resistance that love brings into play is less a political awakening than a primal need to assert the individual's rights in matters of sexual choice and reproduction, regardless of the aims of government, or more radically, the limitations formerly set by biology.

Bibliography

Birnbaum, M., 1966. Aldous Huxley's Animadversions upon Sexual Love. *Texas Studies in Literature and Language*, 8(2), pp.285-296.

Bland, L., 2001. *Banishing the beast: feminism, sex and morality*. London: I B Tauris

Bourke, L., 2018. Sleeps With Monsters: Uplifting Post-apocalypses from Carrie Vaughn. *Tor.Com*. Available at: <https://www.tor.com/2018/08/21/sleeps-with-monsters-uplifting-post-apocalypses-from-carrie-vaughn/> [Accessed: 28/10/2019].

Charnock, A., 2017. *Dreams before the start of time*. Seattle: 47North

Coleman, C. A., 2017. Interview: Carrie Vaughn. *Lightspeed Science Fiction & Fantasy* (86). Available at: <http://www.lightspeedmagazine.com/nonfiction/interview-carrie-vaughn/> [Accessed: 28/10/2019].

Emery, J., 1991. *Rose Macaulay : a writer's life*. London: John Murray.

Galton, F., 1865. Hereditary talent and character Part II. *Macmillan's Magazine*, 12, pp.318-327.

Galton, F., 1908. Local associations for promoting eugenics. *Nature*, 78(2034), pp.645-7.

Galton, F. and Sargent, L. T., 2001. The Eugenic College of Kantsaywhere. *Utopian Studies*, 12(2), pp.191-209.

Garland-Thomson, R., 2012. The case for conserving disability. *Journal of Bioethical Inquiry*, 9(3), pp.339-355.

Gilbert, M., (n.d.) Churchill and Eugenics. *International Churchill Society*. Available at: <https://winstonchurchill.org/publications/finest-hour-extras/churchill-and-eugenics-1/> [Accessed: 28/10/2019].

Gottlieb, E., 2001. *Dystopian fiction East and West : universe of terror and trial*. Montreal ; Ithaca, N.Y.: McGill-Queen's University Press.

Gotto, S., 1917. The eugenic principle in social reconstruction. *The Eugenics review*, 9(3), pp.183-205.

Haldane, J. B. S., 1925. *Daedalus: or Science and the future: a paper read to the Heretics, Cambridge, on February 4th, 1923. Today and tomorrow*. London: Kegan Paul.

Horan, T., 2007. 'Revolutions from the waist downwards: desire as rebellion in Yevgeny Zamyatin's *We*, George Orwell's *1984*, and Aldous Huxley's *Brave New World*', *Extrapolation*, 48(2), pp.314-339.

Huxley, A., 1929. Fashions in love. *Do what you will : essays*. London: Chatto & Windus.

Huxley, A., 1940. 'Introduction', *Hopousia: The sexual and economic foundations of a new society*. New York: O. Piest.

Huxley, A., 1972. *Brave new world revisited. The collected works of Aldous Huxley*. London: Chatto and Windus.

Huxley, A., 2004. *Brave new world*. London: Vintage.

Johnson, K. A., 2016. *China's hidden children: Abandonment, adoption, and the human costs of the One-Child Policy*. University of Chicago Press.

Lonsdale, S., 2019. 'Introduction', *What Not: a prophetic comedy*. Bath: Handheld Press, pp.vii - xxvii.

Macaulay, R., 2019. *What not : a prophetic comedy*. Bath: Handheld Press.

Nadkarni, S., 2018. *Panel Review: Dreams Before the Start of Time by Anne Charnock*: Anglia Ruskin Centre for Science Fiction & Fantasy. Available at: <http://csff-anglia.co.uk/clarke-shadow-jury/shadow-jury-2018/panel-review-dreams-before-the-start-of-time-by-anne-charnock/>   [Accessed: 26/10/2019].

Richardson, A., 2003. *Love and eugenics in the late nineteenth century: rational reproduction and the new woman*. Oxford: Oxford University Press.

Robertson, A., 2017. Bannerless is a post-apocalyptic fantasy about love, murder, and mandatory birth control. *The Verge*. Available at: <https://www.theverge.com/2017/7/12/15905846/bannerless-carrie-vaughn-book-review> [Accessed: 28/10/2019]

Sandel, M. J., 2009. *The case against perfection : ethics in the age of genetic engineering*. Cambridge, Mass: Belknap.

Unwin, J. D., 1940. *Hopousia. The sexual and economic foundations of a new society.* New York: O. Piest.

Vaughn, C., 2016a. Amaryllis. *Amaryllis and other stories*. Bonney Lake, WA: Fairwood Press, pp.290-305.

Vaughn, C., 2016b. Bannerless. *Amaryllis and other stories*. Bonney Lake, WA: Fairwood Press.

Vaughn, C., 2017. *Bannerless*. Boston: Mariner Books/Houghton Mifflin Harcourt.

Vaughn, C., 2018. Carrie Vaughn: Writing the Good Parts. *Locus* (February). Available at: <https://locusmag.com/2018/02/carrie-vaughn-writing-the-good-parts/> [Accessed: 28/10/2019].

Wells, H. G., 2013. The endowment of motherhood. *An Englishman looks at the world: being a series of unrestrained remarks upon contemporary matters*: CreateSpace Independent Publishing Platform, pp.75-76.

Aromanticism, Asexuality, and the Illusion of New Narratives

Lynn O'Connacht

Abstract

In recent years, SFF has made some powerful leaps when it comes to publishing and celebrating diversity, notably in its inclusion of queer characters. While SFF authors have always written such, it is only within the past decade or so that traditional publishing has started to make a concentrated effort to be more deliberately inclusive and diverse.

When it comes to the inclusion of queer characters, however, publishing often seems to focus on queer romance (and implied sexual relationships), leaving other types of relationship behind. Nowhere is this more visible than with asexual or aromantic characters, whose experiences often differ.

Collectively, aromantic and/or asexual characters frequently end the story alone, whereas a demisexual character is almost guaranteed to develop a romantic and sexual relationship. As such, broader trends in the depiction of asexual and aromantic characters in traditional publishing support and maintain the status quo suggesting that romantic (and to a lesser extent sexual) attraction is what makes us human and that non-romantic love continue to be seen as 'lesser' even in contexts that would seem to place it at its highest point.

Yet asexual and especially aromantic narratives offer up a far more nuanced and grander exploration of what it means to be human. The success of Kickstarters focusing on asexual or aromantic relationships shows that the SFF community clearly sees value in the perspectives of these orientations. The purpose of this essay, then, is to explore the way these broader trends about asexuality and aromanticism in SFF inform our understanding of love in general. It is hoped that this paper will encourage people to think about the way aromantic and asexual representation allows us to expand our ideas of what humanity is and how to value love in all its forms.

*

In 2015, the United States Supreme Court made a landmark decision in queer rights, ruling in *Obergefell vs Hodges* that same-sex marriages be licensed and recognised in all US states. While not the first country to legalise same-sex marriage, the social status and clout of the USA in the Western world especially means the ruling was a victory for queer rights worldwide. At the same time, US publishing has slowly started to include more and more openly queer fiction, as can be seen by Malinda Lo's insightful analyses of the rise of YA LGBT fiction for over a decade.

Science fiction and fantasy (SFF) in particular have always dealt with questions of identity, from Shelley's *Frankenstein* (1823) and Le Fanu's *Carmilla* (1872) to Le Guin's *The Left Hand of Darkness* (1969) and C.L. Polk's *Witchmark* (2018). Whether gender identity or sexuality, SFF has always been at the forefront of exploring our understanding of humanity, of what our societies could be like, or what relationships between people may look like. It offers both mirrors and windows, to use R.S. Bishop's metaphor, into experiences not assumed to be the default allonormative[1] cisgender, heterosexual (allocishet

---

1. Allonormativity is the ways in which society has normalised the experience of sexual and romantic attraction. It is an extension of the concepts of heteronormativity and those of compulsory heterosexuality. I prefer the vernacular term 'allosexuality' over academia's frequent 'sexual' and Elizabeth Hanna Hanson's 'eronormativity' as allonormativity incorporates both the eronormativity –the compulsory experience of sexual attraction – that asexuals experience and the amatonormativity – the compulsory

for short) experiences that underlie our understanding of everything from *Snow White*'s happily ever after (1812) to the love triangle in *King Arthur* (12th Century) to the tragic central love relationship in the final season of *Game of Thrones* (2011-2019).

Asexuality and aromanticism have come into our public consciousness as orientations around 2001, though as concepts they have existed since at least the late 19th century. The field of sexology has always had a place for asexuality or, at the very least, potential asexuality (DeLuzio Chasin, Hanson). The aromantic potential is harder to trace, but can still be found in discussions of, for example, romantic friendship and frigidity. While the concept of asexuality has been around in SFF since at least the late 1980s, asexuality and aromanticism as terms did not enter the SFF field until the early 2010s, most notably with Seanan McGuire's *Every Heart a Doorway* (2016). Tracing their potential in earlier works is often hampered by semantics, blurred lines and the usual difficulty of looking at historical queerness through a modern lens. Worse, academic discussions of asexuality and aromanticism often ignore that the terms are, like 'queer', umbrella terms as well as specific identities. Researchers often conflate asexuality with aromanticism, even after explicitly acknowledging them as different concepts, shifting between discussing aromantic asexuality and alloromantic asexuality as suits their argument.

Yet it is through exploring asexuality and aromanticism in their entirety, taking into account the full range of experiences encompassed in these terms, that we can see the vast potential asexuality and aromanticism have to explore what it means to be human and how to value love in all its forms rather than placing romantic and sexual attraction above all others.

---

experience of romantic attraction – that aromantics experience.

What Are Asexuality and Aromanticism?

To discuss asexuality and aromanticism in an academic context, it is important to note that it is only very recently that research has started to see asexuality as a field worth studying. By and large, papers have ignored aromanticism and their definition of asexuality shifts depending on the argument in question. Even Elizabeth Hanson's groundbreaking dissertation *Making Something Out of Nothing* (2013) which aims to present a single, logical framework of asexuality for use in academic theory, is unwittingly inconsistent in its definition. To start, then, this paper will skirt closer to identity politics than may be desirable for the single purpose of showcasing how academia's current definition of asexuality is inadequate to explore asexuality and aromantic theory.

Academia currently does not agree on a single definition of asexuality, though many of the definitions only differ in subtle points. Yet despite taking a variant of 'the non-experience of sexual attraction' (Hanson, 2013) as a definitional starting point, many papers will mention asexual spectrum points, usually demisexuality and greysexuality, in their arguments without pausing to consider what their existence means for the definition of asexuality. Though to date no research into sexuality has presented a satisfactory model, models such as the Kinsey Scale have long since represented sexuality as a spectrum of some variety, usually from heterosexual to homosexual. Given this, it is little surprise to find that asexuality can also be presented as a spectrum and that researchers acknowledge its existence it in their discussions. As an identity, asexuality is more broadly defined as 'having little to no sexual attraction'. Untangling this definition from identity politics and following Hanson's example, a more accurate description of asexuality would be 'the *near*-non-experience of sexual attraction'. This change, though linguistically minor, opens the definition of asexuality up for the nuance that academia has always implicitly relied on.

Likewise, aromanticism can be defined as 'the near-non-experience of romantic attraction'. Academia has, to date, spent little time exploring what the differences between sexual and romantic orientations are, but it is important such a distinction be made. Relying on identity politics for guidance in this instance is futile because the vernacular discussions of asexuality and aromanticism (Przybylo & Cooper, 2014) are just as fraught with disagreement as any other, and a true distinction requires a far more in-depth study of how humanity has defined romance. For example: a candlelit dinner for two is an age-old example of a scene Western society has deemed 'romantic', but why? What about that situation determines that it is coded to be seen as romantic instead of two friends having dinner? For some, it will be the darkness and the intimacy caused the lack of light. For others, it will be the presumed physical proximity caused by a small table. For yet others, it may be the combination of the two or something else entirely. But what, *specifically*, marks those individual elements as 'romantic'? Another example would be kissing. Some people find that kissing, even the kind that exchanges bodily fluids, is firmly romantic in nature, yet others find that it is explicitly sexual in nature. Which of these it is neither academia nor identity politics is currently able to tell us.

For the purposes of this paper, the dividing line between asexuality and aromanticism will be authorial intent. While not a perfect solution by any means, it seems to me the best one. Most traditionally published stories with asexual characters – or with the asexual possibility for them – interweave asexuality and aromanticism in a way that is difficult, if not impossible, to tease out without first creating an entirely new framework for our understanding of human sexuality and relationships. As such, a more subjective and flexible determination of the line between romance and friendship allows a more natural discussion of the texts in question as well as allowing the nuance of the concepts of asexuality and aromanticism to remain intact.

Thus, having concluded that the best dividing line between asexuality and aromanticism is 'intent' for the purposes of this paper, it is time to look at the nuance within the spectrums themselves. Asexuality and aromanticism, seen as spectrums, have many different points on them. This paper, however, will only consider those that have consistently made their way into fictional representation: aromantic asexuality, alloromantic asexuality and alloromantic demisexuality. These can be defined as follows:

Aromantic asexuality: the non-experience of both romantic and sexual attraction

Alloromantic asexuality: the experience of romantic attraction and the non-experience of sexual attraction

Alloromantic demisexuality[2]: the experience of romantic attraction and the near-non-experience of sexual attraction

These are the only three configurations of aromanticism and asexuality currently found in most traditionally published

2. Strictly speaking 'demisexuality' means 'requires a strong emotional bond before developing the capability of sexual attraction', which in novels generally means it is a type of slow-burn romance that takes a long time for the narrative to set up and develop.

SFF novels. Those exceptions that exist often find themselves struggling with the question of queer possibility, especially as it pertains to aromantic asexuality. Ela Przybylo and Danielle Cooper (2014) call these asexual resonances, whereas Hanson (2013) terms this the 'asexual possibility' and discusses the question of how asexuality's invisibility and its tendency to be explained through other means – such as closeted homosexuality – affects the extent to which research can determine whether something is aromantic asexual or not and to what extent we can claim aromantic asexuality is present when it is defined through an *absence*. Contemporary indie novels such as Claudie Arseneault's *Baker Thief* (2018) further complicate matters as these deliberately blur the lines between how readers interpret narratives further, explicitly stating that the goal is to present tropes and ideas related to *romance* through an *aromantic* lens.

As such, this paper restricts its investigation to traditionally published books with explicitly asexual and/or aromantic characters. Focusing on trade publications minimises the impact of identity politics. While trade publishing *does* publish asexual and aromantic characters for the purposes of promoting the interests of asexual and aromantic people, it is often less pronounced than it is in indie publishing. Asexual and aromantic representation in indie publishing is often written by authors who are themselves asexual and/or aromantic and have a strong focus on presenting asexuality and aromanticism as diversely as possible. Restricting the paper to trade publications with confirmed representation also eliminates the question of how absence impacts the asexual possibility in these narratives, though the nature of society's overall understanding of asexuality and aromanticism means that the aromantic possibility is left largely intact even when the asexual possibility has become an asexual certainty. By studying these books with explicit representation, researchers will be able to build a better and more robust framework for asexuality and aromanticism. Hanson's arguments of the stasis of asexuality in narrative terms, for example, are predicated on the complete absence of visible sexual attraction and presents asexuality as an immovable object the narrative falters on, as a story that moves nowhere. Yet this theory remains untested and untried when faced with both a more complete and nuanced understanding of asexuality and aromanticism and a narrative where the absence of sexual or romantic attraction does not produce the issues Hanson's theory would suggest.

General Trends in Asexual and Aromantic Representation

Asexuality and aromanticism are often conflated in fiction – at least until they are not, as my case study of alloromantic asexuality will demonstrate – but before looking at these case studies, it is worth looking at these orientations in SFF fiction as a whole. While the concepts of asexuality and aromanticism have been around for a long time – in modern SFF, they can be traced back as early as Mercedes Lackey's 1985 novella *Swordsworn*[3] – it is only since around 2016 that fiction has seen an increase in deliberate asexual (though not aromantic) representation. Between 2000-2018, traditional SFF publishers published around 31 series and stand-alone novels that feature both the asexual certainty (either through the narrative explicitly describing a character as asexual or through the author confirming it through interviews or speeches) and the asexual possibility (characters which are so strongly coded as

3. The novella seems to have a contested title. I've seen official sources use at least 3 different spellings for the title (Sword-sworn, Swordsworn and Sword Sworn).

asexual it is *almost* a certainty).

It is little surprise that the settings of those narratives that explicitly describe a character as asexual are either contemporary Earth (such as Amanda Ashby's *Demonosity* (2013)) or (far)-future science fiction (Emily Skrutskie's *Hullmetal Girls* (2018)) and that, for the most part, the times when narratives invent their own terms to express (aromantic) asexuality it tends to be within fantasy novels (Sherwood Smith's *Banner of the Damned* (2012)). Within fantasy especially, it has long been a question what words can/cannot be used within the setting with many readers complaining, sometimes loudly, that words do not 'fit' within the artificial cultural bounds conjured by the setting. While this extends all the way to modern phrasings such as "Yo, what up!", it also includes using terms such as 'homosexual' or 'asexual', as these are deemed anachronistic in a fantasy setting presumably inspired and building upon a medieval understanding of the world. Such books may come up with their own terminology to convey these concepts without risking breaking the reader's immersion. Science fiction and contemporary fantasy, understandably, has few such concerns.

Within SFF, one can already begin to trace stereotypes and narrative tropes pertaining to asexual and aromantic narratives. Often these tropes map onto the stereotypes of asexuality and aromanticism, presenting the characters as in some way isolated from society or as outright aliens or robots specifically because they are not human. Two prominent examples of this are Commander Data and Seven of Nine from *Star Trek: The Next Generation* (1987-1994) and *Star Trek: Voyager* (1995-2001) respectively. Data is an android who cannot experience human emotions, such as love, and much of his narrative is devoted to becoming more human. He even has an episode dedicated to attempting to engage in a romantic relationship and failing. Seven, meanwhile, is human but has been assimilated by the Borg, leading to emotional restrictions that affect her understanding of romance and her lack of sexual attraction, as noted by Mia Consalvo in "Borg Babes, Drones, and the Collective: Reading Gender and the Body in Star Trek". Though it is far from the main focus of her narrative, attempting to understand romance and attraction are a key part of Seven's rehumanisation throughout the story. Both these narratives are examples of an allonormative worldview, presenting sex and, particularly, romance as necessary experiences for a character to be considered fully human by the narrative if not the characters around them[4].

Social isolation is also a frequent companion for asexual or aromantic characters, such as Clariel's stated disinterest in human society in Garth Nix's *Clariel* (2014) and her subsequent exile from the kingdom at the end of the novel. This trope also features in Sherwood Smith's *Banner of the Damned*, (2012), R.J. Anderson's *Quicksilver* (2013), Elizabeth Bear's *Jacob's Ladder* series (2007-2011), Mackenzi Lee's *The Lady's Guide to Petticoats and Piracy* (2018), and Martha Wells' *Murderbot* series[5] (2017 to present).

To date, few papers discussing asexuality and aromanticism in literature have been published. Hanson's *Making Something Out of Nothing* (2013) was the first major examination of asexuality in fiction, posing the theory that asexuality is akin to 'stasis', that it disrupts the narrative of desire. To Hanson, it is a foregone conclusion that 'desire', even narrative desire,

---

4. *The Next Generation* has an entire episode, "The Measure of a Man", dedicated to determining whether Data is a person in his own right.

5. This series also features the robotic aromantic and asexual trope as Murderbot is a type of robot. Though Wells has mentioned that Murderbot is not intended to be asexual or aromantic representation, some readers recommend it for that.

must be sexual in nature, saying "And as modern subjects, we reflexively presume a sexual basis to desire, such that the accounts of narrative available to us are implicitly incompatible with asexuality" (p.214). While an understandable argument, it is one that reinforces the (het)eronormativity (Hanson) and allonormativity within our society. Rather than creating a framework in which asexuality and aromanticism are relegated to the outside, I seek to create a framework that stands free of the restrictions imposed by allonormativity. There is no conflict between asexuality, aromanticism and 'desire' once one dissolves the Freudian idea that everything must be sexual in nature.

Asexuality and aromanticism as they are depicted in traditional SFF publishing today by and large supports the framework of allonormativity rather than undermining it, as the examination of Garth Nix's *Clariel* (2014), R.J. Anderson's *Quicksilver* (2013) and Tim Pratt's *The Wrong Stars* (2017) will show. Though depictions of these orientations have the power to challenge how we view the fabric and structure of society, traditional publishing rarely, if ever, takes the chance to explore these narratives, shifting asexual and aromantic ideas and concepts into a strictly allonormative coat.

Aromantic Asexuality in *Clariel*

The eponymous Clariel in Garth Nix's 2014 YA prequel to the Abhorsen series has been confirmed as aroace by the author in a Reddit AMA, though her orientations are only (strongly) hinted at in the narrative. It is a highly controversial book among the asexual and aromantic communities, with readers either loving the representation in it or finding it deeply offensive. *Clariel*'s narrative is a villain's origin story. It is a story of vengeance, but also one of good intentions going wrong and of making bad choices for the right reasons.

When the book begins, Clariel simply wants to return to the place she considers home. Finding herself pressed into a life she emphatically does not want, she struggles to find a way to assert her own personality and take control of her own life. Clariel, having grown up in a small town near a great forest, is not used to the bustle of the city. Yet as a relative of both the king and the Abhorsen, Clariel soon finds herself embroiled in the city's politics and her life turned upside-down as her parents are murdered. Seeking immediate vengeance, Clariel struggles to escape the confinement placed on her by her grandfather, the current Abhorsen, and finds herself accepting the aid of Free Magic creatures to escape[6]. They, however, have agendas of their own and, betrayed, Clariel comes to realise how they used her yearning for freedom and desire for justice to manipulate her. The novel ends with her connection to magic artificially severed and her exile from the kingdom. The author's note at the end remarks that Clariel will go on to become Chlorr of the Mask, one of the main antagonists in the original trilogy and in the series capstone, *Goldenhand*.

From this brief summary one can already see the main strand of criticism levelled against the book: it ends with Clariel not only exiled from the kingdom forever, but her narrative will continue on with her becoming a necromancer using Free Magic and becoming an undead antagonist of the original trilogy. This narrative ending fits in with the stereotype that asexual and aromantic people do not have a place within society because they do not follow allonormative and amatonormative ways.

Clariel's asexuality is hinted at a number of times throughout

6. Free Magic, the novel mentions several times, is inimical to life, something Clariel's innate empathy questions multiple times throughout the novel.

the narrative, most notably when she rebuffs Belatiel's clear attraction to her, saying "But in any case, let me say again to be perfectly clear, I am not interested in jumping into bed with you or anyone, or sighing and cooing and playing at romance, or planning a marriage or any of it. But I do value you as a good friend. All right?" (Nix, 2014, Chapter 21)

Though Clariel's asexuality and aromanticism are clear in their descriptions and she has been confirmed as aromantic asexual, the novel never uses those exact words. Instead, the book uses the concept of a 'natural singleton', which it explains as being "like the russet martens who only came together for the briefest mating season and then went their own way". (Chapter 1)

Clariel, it must be said, is not presented as unsympathetic. She is shown to be capable of deep empathy, such as when she abandons her plan to escape to the Great Forest because doing so puts Belatiel in danger. It is also shown, less favourably, at the start of the novel when she releases Aziminil before Kargrin can capture it out of an understanding of what it is like to feel trapped. Yet the novel repeatedly thwarts her desires and good intentions – arguably the asexual possibility described by Hanson at work – and ultimately sees her cast out of society entirely, her only escape from being sentenced to death coming from Belatiel's romantic/sexual attraction to her. Though the novel does not outright say that Bel saves her because he loves her – instead he says he promised he'd help her escape – the epilogue still makes these feelings clear in a brief exchange:

> If you could stay . . . I would still want to . . . well, you know how I feel."
> "I know," said Clariel. She stood up and went over to him, lightly touching his own cheek, smooth under her hand.

"Marry Denima, Bel. You'd be good for each other." (Nix, 2014, Epilogue)

Throughout the novel, Clariel finds herself torn from her place in society more and more. It begins before the novel does, with her family having moved from Estwael into Belisaere, then continues with Clariel losing both her parents, then her connection to Charter Magic and, ultimately, her place in society as a whole as she gets exiled far beyond the borders of the realm governed by Charter Magic.

Charter Magic is a specific kind of magic, a restrained and ordered kind of magic, a civilising aspect that made not only society possible but life itself. It is contrasted by all the magic that could not or did not fit within the Charter. Throughout *Clariel* much is made of the way in which people connect to this Charter. Like all members of the Abhorsen bloodline, Clariel has access to it, though her usage of Free Magic weakens this link considerably, ultimately being wholly severed.

> Clariel hesitated, then tried to reach for the Charter, to conjure a simple light. It was the first spell she'd learned, something she knew well, and she could nearly always make it work. But the Charter wasn't there, or she could no longer feel its presence. Yet she knew it was everywhere, the Charter made up all things, it described the world and everything in it . . . Except Free Magic. That was outside the Charter.
> "But I wore the robe, the mask . . ." whispered Clariel. She touched her forehead Charter mark again, and once more reached for the Charter. This time, she felt it, but far away. No great drift of marks fell upon her; they stayed as distant as the stars above, and just as out of reach. But even that far-off, momentary glimpse relieved Clariel. She had never really valued the Charter, neither understood it nor wanted to know

more, but she felt its absence keenly.
It felt wrong, unnatural. (Nix, 2014, Chapter 29)

Clariel's relationship to Free Magic and Charter Magic mirrors the ways in which she loses her connection with the world around her. As her bonds to other people loosen or fall away in death, her bonds to the society and world made possible by the Charter start to fall away, aligning her more and more with the Free Magic so reviled within the setting. While it is obvious that Clariel does not value this connection deeply until it is lost, she *does* value it and does not want to lose it. "If there was a means to regain her connection to the Charter then using Free Magic was an acceptable risk," (ibid) the narrative explains.

Clariel's journey is one of trying to find one's place in society and discovering that it does not exist. That society, explicitly, does not want to accept her as she is. From her parents who refuse to let her follow her dreams, to the schoolmistress unable to see just how important those dreams are to her, to the Abhorsen who tries to lock her up for her own good, to the Free Magic creatures that manipulate her for their own purposes, to the queen who ultimately wants to sentence her to death. The only time society seems able to accept even the idea of Clariel is when the narrative brings up Belatiel's feelings for her, and even then this acceptance is conditional on her confirming to allonormativity. Belatiel will help her escape, but only if she first tries to fit in with the world around her. Only after Clariel has made the effort to be something she is not can she get the aid she needs.

If Hanson's logic of asexuality assumes that asexuality is always something outside of the narrative that thwarts its natural progression, then the plot progression of *Clariel* is the more substantive version of this theory. The romantic arc between Belatiel and Clariel ultimately goes nowhere, after all. Clariel herself, though alive, is forced to abandon everything she has ever known and her story left open-ended. Though the author's note tells us that she will become Chlorr, the reader is denied the exploration of how Clariel assumes this identity, leaving a gap in her story across the series. Aromantic asexuality in fiction, then, presents as a disconnect from society and an inability to fit within it.

Alloromantic Asexuality in *Quicksilver*

Characters such as Clariel stand in stark contrast to characters such as Tori, from R.J. Anderson's *Quicksilver* (2013). In R.J. Anderson's companion novel/sequel to *Ultraviolet* (2011), the narrative follows Tori. In *Ultraviolet*, Tori is seemingly disintegrated during a fight with the protagonist Alison. However, things are not what they seem, and in *Quicksilver* Tori takes the lead as she and her family have gone into hiding to escape persecution. They have assumed fake identities and Tori has found herself forcibly cut off from fully interacting with society.

Unlike the aromantic asexual arc severing the character from society, Tori's alloromantic asexual arc is one of reintegration into allonormative society. Though she starts out artificially separated from society, the novel is focused on her finding ways to reintegrate with it, seeking out connections with one of her coworkers, joining the makerspace, even teaming up with Alison to foil the antagonist's plans to such an extent that Tori can return to living a life set within allonormative boundaries, with a romantic kiss between her and Milo becoming the culmination of her narrative.

It is again this final scene where the narrative's adherence to allonormativity is clearest. Throughout the novel, Tori has made it clear that she is asexual, but the narrative falls into the common trap of assuming that "asexual" means "aromantic asexual", at least up until the moment that it does not. Throughout the book, Tori is vocal about her lack of sexual attraction and what that means for her social relationships. The narrative also depicts her as having no romantic interests in anyone (until it does), conflating aromanticism and asexuality in a way that can be difficult to untangle.

In our current Western understanding of sexuality as a whole, the concepts of sexual and romantic attraction are fundamentally linked. Roughly, the idea is that if you are sexually attracted to X, then you are also romantically attracted to X, or vice versa. We can see this concept at work in many models of a sexuality continuum drawn between homosexuality and heterosexuality. Yet an alloromantic asexual – someone who experiences romantic but not sexual attraction – by their very existence already tells us that something is going on.

For fiction, the grand question is how to portray this effectively, and it is often done through the way demonstrated in *Quicksilver*: Tori is never shown to want to engage in any kind of romantic behaviour with her love interest *until* near the end.

The reader's introduction to Milo happens early on in part one, when Tori is waiting for a bus. Her description of Milo is almost functional in nature, saying "He had feathery black hair, cat's eyes behind rectangular glasses, and a pair of earbuds tucked into the collar of his jacket. Like Jon and most of the other part-timers, he was around my age, and I was pretty sure he'd been at the store at least as long as I had." (Anderson, 2013, Part 1)

Allosexual romance narratives frequently have some kind of physical reaction or other indication that the character is affected by their love interest's physical presence. Compare the citation above to the way the narrative in *Hush, Hush* by Becca Fitzpatrick first introduces the love interest, Patch.

> He sat slouched one table back, cool black eyes holding a steady gaze forward. Just like always. I didn't for one moment believe he just sat there, day after day, staring into space. He was thinking something, but instinct told me I probably didn't want to know what.
>
> (…)
>
> His black eyes sliced into me, and the corners of his mouth tilted up. My heart fumbled a beat and in that pause, a feeling of gloomy darkness seemed to slide like a shadow over me. It vanished in an instant, but I was still staring at him. His smile wasn't friendly. It was a smile that spelled trouble. With a promise. (Fitzpatrick, 2010, Chapter 1)

Note that where Anderson's focus is on making sure the reader knows the basics necessary to picture Milo, it is a broad-strokes description more concerned with making sure readers know what his place in the setting is. Patch's introduction is narrow. The reader learns nothing about him save that he has black hair and an unfriendly smile. Fitzpatrick's focus is on those aspects of Patch's appearance that immediately stand out to Nora and, crucially, how she reacts to them physically: her heart skips a beat.

Alloromantic asexual narratives are not devoid of descriptions of aesthetic appreciation or attraction. One such example can be seen in Seanan McGuire's *Every Heart a Doorway* when Nancy describes her attraction to Kade.

> Nancy set her hand in the crook of his elbow, feeling the traitorous red creeping back into her cheeks. This was always the difficult part, back when she'd been at her old school: explaining that "asexual" and "aromantic" were different things. She *liked* holding hands and trading kisses. She'd had several boyfriends in elementary school, just like most of the other girls, and she had always found those practice relationships completely satisfying. It wasn't until puberty had come along and changed the rules that she'd started pulling away in confusion and disinterest. Kade was possibly the most beautiful boy she'd ever seen. She wanted to spend hours sitting with him and talking about pointless things. She wanted to feel his hand against her skin, to know that his presence was absolute and focused entirely on her. The trouble was, it never seemed to end there, and that was as far as she was willing to go. (McGuire, 2016, Chapter 6)

Yet there is a distinct lack of focus on physical attraction in many asexual narratives. McGuire's description of Kade's physical appearance is simply 'beautiful'. There is no indication of what, exactly, Nancy finds so beautiful. The same is true of Tori's descriptions of Milo throughout *Quicksilver*.

It is not only with Tori's descriptions of Milo that the reader can see the differences between an asexual worldview and an allosexual one, however. About a third of the way through the book, Alison's description of her boyfriend as 'sexy' completely throws Tori.

> 'Sorry, what?' I couldn't have heard her right. Had she actually said *sexy*?
> She blushed. Yes, she had.
> And there it was again. The feeling that came over me every

time this subject came up, as though I was standing on one side of some vast and uncrossable abyss and everybody else I knew was waving at me from the other. Until two hours ago I'd thought it had something to do with the chip in my arm, but since Sebastian had a chip as well, I guessed not. (Anderson, 2013, Interlude (2.3))

In full context, Alison is remarking that she finds her boyfriend's name sexy because of her synaesthesia. While this would lend itself towards confusion for any character due to a lack of understanding of synaesthesia, Anderson quickly ties Tori's understanding not to how a synesthete experiences the world, but to how her specific experience differs from that of others.

Quicksilver's Tori is, quite literally, an alien entity that was raised believing she was human and as part of her initial introduction the reader learns that, while she is innately good with machines, *people* do not come easily to her. People skills are something she had to learn, slotting her firmly into the general stereotype people have about asexuals as disinterested in and unskilled at social interactions of any kind and about asexuals as being inhuman due to their lack of sexual attraction.

Quicksilver is also quick to undermine both these allonormative assumptions, however. As can be seen in the citation above, Sebastian – who is an alien like Tori – does experience sexual attraction, and moreover he is not as terrible at people skills as Tori is. Her alienness, then, is not implicitly linked to her asexuality and the narrative as a whole undermines the idea that Tori is an outsider in society.

True, she and her parents are living in hiding to protect her and she starts the narrative off deliberately isolating herself from the world around her, but the story is focused on allowing

Tori to reach out to others. Despite her self-imposed isolation, she becomes good friends with Milo, for example, and she reconnects with Alison and Sebastian. Against her parents' wishes she finds a way to join a makerspace, a club where she can pursue both social interaction and her love of machinery at the same time. Tori's alloromantic asexual narrative is about reclaiming her identity and finding her place within the world.

Demisexuality in *The Wrong Stars*

Tim Pratt's *The Wrong Stars* (2017) is the first book in a space operatic adventure series starring a demisexual lead. It is, currently and to my knowledge, the only traditionally published SFF novel with an explicitly demisexual character. In *The Wrong Stars*, Callie and her crew are out salvaging when they discover a 500-year-old ship where someone, Elena, is held in cryosleep. Mysteriously, this ship is missing most of its crew and has clearly seen strange repairs. It also should not have been where it was discovered. Upon being awakened, Elena exclaims that her crew have made first contact with an alien race and that the rest of her crew needs help. The romantic arc of the book is a B-plot to the *Firefly*-style action and focuses on Elena, who is either bisexual or pansexual, and Callie, who is explicitly demisexual. At least two out of its core cast of secondary characters are also coded to be read as both asexual and aromantic.

The Wrong Stars, however, falls into the same trap of depiction that much current demisexual representation seems to fall into, which is that the narrative confuses limited lust-at-first-sight with needing an emotional bond before experiencing attraction at all. The book introduces Callie's identity by having an AI imprint of her ex-husband's mind tell Elena that

"Back in the days when she had a dating profile on the Tangle, Callie identified as demisexual. She's attracted to people she develops feelings for, whether they're femme, butch, andro, enby, genderfluid, shifting, or otherwise. Attraction follows interest, for her. I think you interest her greatly." (Pratt, 2017, Chapter 18). While the first half of the definition is fine, if somewhat imprecise, the second half fails to define 'interest' in any meaningful way and leaves the reader leeway to ignore the necessary absence of primary attraction. In certain versions of the split attraction model proposed by ace activists, attraction is divided into primary and secondary attraction. Ace activist Julie Sondra Decker explains primary and secondary attraction in *The Invisible Orientation*, saying:

> We all know it's possible for some people to be immediately sexually attracted to other people based on information gathered with one's physical senses—without knowing anything about their personalities. It can be based on looks or voice or chemistry or charisma, and it's known as a **primary sexual attraction** reaction. That person seems like a good sex partner, and there's a physical and/or mental sexual reaction. It doesn't mean one is necessarily *realistically* interested in sex with that person or is ready to run into the nearest closet for a quickie. It just means there is a reaction that is sexual—that a person can be seen in a sexual context even as a stranger.
>
> **Secondary sexual attraction** is more gradual, though not inherently a "different kind" of sexual attraction—it just happens under different circumstances. A partner starts to seem sexually appealing only after an emotional bond develops (not necessarily love), based on qualities that can't be perceived through immediate observation of the subject without interaction. This can happen in conjunction with

primary sexual attraction, combining with it, enhancing it. But some people *only* experience that slow, less reactionary rise of interest—they never experience primary or immediate sexual attraction and can't feel attraction to strangers or celebrities they don't know. (Decker, 2014, Part 2, original emphasis)

The first introduction of Callie's attraction to Elena occurs in chapter 1. In this, her crew member Ashok has called out to her to look at one of the cryopods.

"There's someone on ice over here." Ashok stood by the last container, its glowing blue control panel casting weird shadows on his already weird face. "Most of the power on the ship has been diverted to maintaining life support and keeping this pod functional, I think."
Callie joined him and looked into the pod. There was a window over the inhabitant's face, and the glass wasn't even foggy or covered in ice, the way cryopod windows inevitably appeared in historical immersives. Artistic license. The figure inside was a petite woman with straight black hair, dressed in white coveralls. She looked like a sleeping princess (peasant garb aside), and something in Callie sparkled at the sight of her. *Uh oh*, she thought.
"Can we wake her up?" she said. Not with a kiss, of course. This wasn't a fairy tale, despite the glass casket.
(Pratt, 2017, Chapter 1, original emphasis)

The trouble with this passage, of course, is that since it says *something* sparkled in Callie, and the narrative never defines this particular something, one could make an argument that Callie's clear primary attraction – after all, she knows nothing more about Elena than that she's pretty at this point – is romantic rather than sexual in nature, but the allonormative environment this is written in, coupled with Callie's thoughts immediately jumping to the idea of waking Elena with a kiss, suggests that Callie's 'something' is specifically sexual attraction. Moreover, in the beginning of chapter 3, Callie does explicitly refer to it as attraction and attributes it, specifically, to lust.

> Doctor Oh was watchful and serious, and seemed very self-contained. Callie felt that sparkle again, a throb in her solar plexus, a tightness in her chest, the desire to say *oh oh oh*. She resolved to ignore the attraction. They'd been cooped up on the *Raven* too long, doing speed-runs to the Jovian Imperative and back, and Elena was the first person other than her crew and Europan dock workers she'd seen in weeks. What she felt was just the lust of deprivation. And perhaps a touch of space madness. (Pratt, 2017, Chapter 3)

Here Callie explicitly describes a physical reaction in response to Elena's physical appearance, specifically her bearing, as attraction and 'the lust of deprivation', ending up conflating libido with attraction.

Callie, then, though clearly described as demisexual, follows a narrative line that is firmly in keeping with allonormative experiences and expectancies. She experiences *some* form of physical attraction to Elena at first sight and her romantic narrative arc is about nurturing and growing that initial attraction into something stronger.

Callie and her crew are, to some extent, outcasts from society and serve as a found family for one another. None of them appear to have strong roots to the community on Meditreme Station, though all of them work within the confines of the Trans-Neptunian Authority, performing everything from law enforcement jobs to freight haul, and have friends on the station. When, in the course of the plot, their home is lost – fitting with the tropes of asexual isolation – Callie is never truly alone or cut off from society. She has her found family and she sets out to discover who is responsible for the murder of so many people, but she always remains connected to society. She may be on the outskirts, but her demisexual arc is never one of either rejecting or seeking integration into society.

Conclusion

Though this paper only covers a handful of examples in detail, these patterns can be traced in numerous books with asexual spectrum characters in them. Aromantic asexual narratives, such as in *Clariel* (2014), are about the character rejecting society and social contacts. Two other such examples would be Seanan McGuire's *Every Heart a Doorway* (2016) or Alyssa Wong's *You'll Surely Drown Here, If You Stay* (2016), both following the same motifs linking aromanticism and asexuality to death and exile from society.

Alloromantic asexual narratives, such as in *Quicksilver*, (2013) are about the character finding a way to be reintegrated into society. Other examples include *Keeper of the Dawn* by Dianna Gunn (2017) and *We Awaken* by Calista Lynne (2016), both following the same motifs of an outsider finding a place within the dominant society through a romantic relationship.

Demisexual narratives, such as in *The Wrong Stars* (2017), mimic allosexual narratives with the character already a part of society. Another example of demisexuality in narrative would be Sherwood Smith and Rachel Manija Brown's *The Change* series, starting with *Stranger* (2014).

In this way, the combination of these arcs demonstrates that our current depiction and use of asexuality and aromanticism in fiction works to maintain allonormativity, notably the amatonormative aspect of it, rather than examining new ways to explore our humanity and our understanding of the world around us. Despite the seeming acceptance of other relationships or narrative structures, experiencing sexual and especially romantic feelings is still depicted as central to people's place within society as a whole. These arcs present people who do not experience romantic attraction as such undesirable members of society that they must be cast out, voluntarily or forcefully, as demonstrated by the ending of *Clariel*. These threads posit that experiencing romantic attraction allows one to be (re)integrated into society as well as that this integration is desirable, such as seen at the end of *Quicksilver*. Demisexuality is shown to be little different from allosexuality, though with a dearth of demisexual characters in SFF, researchers would be wise to include contemporary romance as well.

Yet, despite the predictability of how asexual and aromantic narratives are structured to uphold allonormativity, asexuality and aromanticism are ideally poised to challenge the ideas of what love entails and who, ultimately, is allowed to participate fully in our societies. These orientations offer us tools to examine in more detail than ever before the alloromantic and allosexual concepts that society has enshrined. Marriage equality, for example, does not lead to widescale legal protection. The media focuses deeply on nuclear (often heterosexual) families, leaving other arrangements, at best, subtext. Exploring the way asexual and aromantic ideas challenge allonormativity in fiction allows us to imagine a future where everyone can be a part of society just the way they are.

Bibliography

Anderson, R.J., 2013. *Quicksilver*. [EPUB] Sydney: Orchard Books. Available at: Kobo <https://www.kobo.com/> [Accessed March 15 2020].

Arseneault, C., 2018. *Baker Thief*. [Kindle MOBI] The Kraken Collective. Available at: Amazon.com <https:// www.amazon.com> [Accessed March 15 2020].

Consalvo, M., 2004. Borg Babes, Drones, and The Collective: Reading Gender and the Body in Star Trek. *Women's Studies in Communication*, 27(2), pp.177-203.

Decker, J.S., 2014. *The Invisible Orientation*. [Kindle MOBI] New York City: Carrel Books. Available at: Amazon.com <https:// www.amazon.com> [Accessed March 15 2020].

DeLuzio Chasin, C.J., 2011. Theoretical Issues in the Study of Asexuality. *Archives of Sexual Behavior*, 40(4), pp.713-723.

Fitzpatrick, B., 2010. *Hush, Hush*. [Kindle MOBI] New York: Simon & Schuster Books for Young Readers. Available at: Amazon.com <https:// www.amazon.com> [Accessed March 15 2020].

Hanson, E., 2013. *Making Something Out of Nothing: Asexuality and Narrative*. Ph.D. Loyola University Chicago.

Lo, M., 2019. *A Decade of LGBTQ YA Since Ash — Malinda Lo*. [online] Malinda Lo. Available at: <https://www.malindalo.com/blog/2019/3/18/a-decade-of-lgbtq-ya-since-ash> [Accessed 10 Oct. 2019].

McGuire, S., 2016. *Every Heart a Doorway*. [Kindle MOBI] New York: Tom Doherty Associates. Available at: Amazon.com <https:// www.amazon.com> [Accessed March 15 2020].

Nix, G., 2014. *Clariel*. [EPUB] Sydney: Allen & Unwin. Available at: Kobo <https://www.kobo.com/> [Accessed March 15 2020].

Nix, G., 2019. *I'm author Garth Nix, here to talk books and writing including my new Old Kingdom book GOLDENHAND. AMA! : books*. [online] Reddit. com. Available at: <https://www.reddit.com/r/books/comments/55uhg6/im_author_garth_nix_here_to_talk_books_and/d8dr8cx/> [Accessed 10 Oct.

2019].

Pratt, T., 2017. *The Wrong Stars*. [EPUB] London: Angry Robot. Available at: Kobo <https://www.kobo.com/> [Accessed March 15 2020].

Przybylo, E. and Cooper, D., 2014. Asexual Resonances: Tracing a Queerly Asexual Archive. GLQ: *A Journal of Lesbian and Gay Studies*, 20(3), pp.297-318.

Star Trek: The Next Generation. 1987-1994. [TV programme]. USA: CBN.

Star Trek: Voyager. 1995-2001. [TV programme]. USA: UPN.

Shades of Unrequieted love. Demon tears and amour de loin in Japanese anime and manga

Steph P. Bianchini

Abstract

The trope of unrequited love in its many declinations has crossed centuries, literatures and genres; it is therefore not surprising to find it well represented in the Japanese manga and anime popular culture.

Unrequired love with demonic traits is at the very centre of *Devilman* [デビルマン], one of the most iconic manga /anime ever (both in its original manga version 1970s by Go Nagai and more recently as the Netflix reboot *Devilman Crybaby*), which offers also an example of queer love surprisingly modern for the times of its original creation. This subtrope would remain in the manga tradition to resurface with similar relationship traits but more complex dynamics and even darker tones in another (still ongoing) manga/anime blockbuster of the 1990s: Kentaro Miura's *Berserk* [ベルセルク], to which the last section of this study is devoted.

Different in content and tones but otherwise related is Riyoko Ikeda's most notable creation, the historical manga /anime *Versailles no Bara* [ベルサイユのばら], also known as *Lady Oscar* or *La Rose de Versailles*. One of the bestselling *shojo* manga of all time, *Versailles no Bara* is tragic love Japanese-style at its purest definition, which has made generations of fans, young and adult, cry. It also reflects, in its featured relationships, aspects of the troubadours' amour de loin, where the sentiment of love becomes an impossible dream worth dying for.

*

How hearts break and (rarely) mend in Japanese anime and manga. An introduction.

The present article is an analysis of unrequired love[1] in Japanese anime and manga, which focuses on a few specific aspects of the trope using three case studies: *Devilman* (1972-1973), *Versailles no Bara* (1972-73) and *Berserk* (1989-present). The aspects here considered for analysis are subtropes of unrequited love as a whole, and they are demonic love – one of the lovers or would-be lovers presents an inhuman and/or evil nature – and *amour de loin* as defined in the *Troubadour* tradition.

The article will also consider the presence of queer/genderfluid love, given the relevance it plays in manga/anime culture, starting with the ideal of androgynous beauty (*bishonen*), albeit both are more typical of a specific audience[2] (*shojo*)[3] than a character of the mangaverse as a whole.

---

1. In this article, 'unrequited' is used in the meaning of '*not reciprocated or returned in kind*' (Merriam-Webster, 2020, online); the reasons this happens, however, can be quite different, and they might be not only due to genuine lack of interest but also to external obstacles, incapability of expressing their own feelings or even to understand them, denial. The love relationships analysed here span across them all.

2. Manga/anime are classified according to their intended audience, which also explains why some of them are more graphic in content and present dark themes and philosophies. *Shonen* are aimed at male teens between 12-18 years old, while their respective feminine are called *shojo*. All mecha (such as the *Gundam* franchise and *Attack of Titan*) are generally *shonen*, and most of the action-themed series as well, even though some of them, due to their violence and dark tones like the world-famous *First of the North Star* (also known as *Okuto-no-Ken*) are borderline in the adult (male) audience, called instead *seinen*. Of the manga/anime analysed in this article, two are *seinen* (*Devilman* and *Berserk*) and one is a *shojo* (*Versailles-no-Bara*).

3. "While S-kankei have become less common in postwar Japan where co-ed schooling is the norm and dating is no longer forbidden, girls' preference for homogender romance remains. Those pre-war magazines were gradually replaced post-war by *shôjo* manga, but instead of girl-girl stories, we now have bishônen, shônen-ai, and yaoi, all stories of love between beautiful, feminine-looking boys." (Shamoon, 2009, online)

The three series singled out for analysis have been chosen with a specific reason in mind: while they are not the only ones developing the above-mentioned aspects, all three

(1) have become iconic and influential in portraying them;

(2) are related to each other, either in terms of themes (*Devilman* as the obvious precursor for *Berserk*) or inspiration (Miura, *Berserk*'s creator, listed *Versailles no Bara* as one of his references).

This analysis does not aim at any claim of being complete or exhaustive.

There are many other series worth of in-depth treatment when the trope unrequired love is discussed, and that have been left out for reasons of space, first of all, *Gundam*. A franchise consisting of 43 instalments (so far) over 40 years of existence[4], *Gundam* has portrayed a vast series of love dynamics that are never simple and seldom happy, from star-crossed lovers (Amuro Rey and Lala San [*1979 Mobil Suit Gundam*]; Camille Bidan and Four [*Gundam Z*]) to unrequited love of the purest tradition (Hataway Bryte for Quess Paraya [*Char Counter-attack*]; Reccoa and Haman Karn for Char [*Gundam Z*]; Mashymre Cello for Haman Karn [*Gundam ZZ*]) and with characters ranging from delusional (Quess Paraya) to manipulative (Char; Paptimus Scirocco [*Gundam Z*][5]) to hopelessly in love.

However, of all manga/anime series (or franchise, as it is the case here), *Gundam* is one of the less queer and genderfluid

4. *Gundam* is well-known among the fandom as a franchise with especially dark tones for a mecha series (therefore targeting MG or early teens). This darkness is more evident in some of the earliest instalments, even though some most recent series – like *Gundam Ironblood Orphans* – have shown the same sombre atmosphere of *Gundam Z* and *Gundam Victory*.

5. Scirocco can be considered a darker version of the iconic Char 'Red Comet' when women are about.

overall[6] and, considering how important is this aspect in the other three examples studies in this article, it weighted against its inclusion.

A last word about trigger warnings.

Due to some of the content covered in the following sections, content warnings have been given in footnotes.

Satan in Love: demonic devotion and cosmic cruelty[7]

Devilman [デビルマン] (1972-1973), Go Nagai's most iconic and well-known creation, combines Western literature (Go Nagai is a reader of Dante's *Commedia* and has even authored a previous manga, *Demon Lord Dante – Mao Dante* [魔王ダンテ[8]] (2002), demonology and Japanese folklore[9] with Lacanian undertones[10]). One of earliest manga/anime to reach the

---

6. It doesn't mean there are no examples, only that they remain at a platonic level, even in the way they're worded and experienced, in a marked difference to what is discussed here. *Gundam Wing* is one that more have made concession to the *shojo* tropes and audience – to the point that fan fiction has long speculated (and written) about Heero and Duo, Trewa and Quatre, and Treize and Zech in terms of romantic involvement.

7. [Content Warning: I'd say that overall *Devilman* is more nihilistic than disturbing, at least today after forty years of violent, dark manga, but there are, especially in the final chapters, violent and graphic scenes. It doesn't help that it ends with a literal apocalypse.]

8. "I tend to think I was greatly influenced by my first images of devils – Gustave Dore's illustrations of Satan trapped in ice in Dante's Inferno. It had inspired Mao Dante and went on to influence Devilman too," (Nagai, 2006, online)

9. "Human-demon transformation are a stock theme of ukiyo-e painting," (Gill, 1998, p. 45).

10. It could be repeated for *Devilman* what Souvilay said about *Neon Genesis Evangelion*: [it] "superpose ainsi trois formes de construction du sens: science-fiction, ésotérisme et psychanalyse" (Suvilay, 2017, p. 7), with the addition of a strong component of horror. Mangas and anime often provide rich opportunities in this sense, and, in this specific instance, for a Jungian

Western audience, it has known in the 40 years of its existence many adaptations, sequels and reboots[11]. It embodies tropes that have later become common in manga /anime. The analysis here follows the storyline of the original manga, making some passing reference to the recent Netflix's anime adaptation *Devilman Crybaby* (2018) by director Masaaki Yuasa, disregarding the original anime and being quite different in character and tones[12].

In the manga we have a triad of characters and two main relationships, which inform the whole story: the first one is the couple Akira Fudo (the protagonist) and Miki Makamoto, (even though Miki is Akira's cousin and they have grown up together, which complicates the story). At the moment Akira becomes Devilman, however, things start drifting apart, as Akira is taken away to a darker world where Miki has no place. This doesn't

---

(*Berserk*) and Lacanian (*Devilman*) analysis. For instance, Lacan's linkage between the 'other' as something escaping our comprehension, demons as the 'other' *par excellence*, and love/desire (Lacan 1966) is apparent in Go Nagai's universe.

11. For the spin-off list, see: <https://www.animenewsnetwork.com/ encyclopedia/manga.php?id=2454>.

12. This is due to the unusual way *Devilman* was conceived, and nobody tells it better than the author himself: "I initially conceived Devilman as a TV animation series. A producer for TOEI Animation Co., Ltd. who had read Mao Dante, wondered if I could come up with an animation series with a devil – albeit a very human one – as its hero. Thus Devilman was born, an amalgam of Devil and man with bat wings as his trademark. [...] The TV and manga versions of Devilman began around the same time. But due to my particular creative method, the two works ended up being very different. The basic concept for the TV series was simple: Evil vs. Evil, revolving around a hero. Evil takes over a human body, and to protect Miki, the girl he loves, the hero participates in the human world and battles evil. The magazine series, on the other hand, grew further from this plot with each episode. One reason for the difference in the two versions is that the readership of Shukan Shonen Magazine was consistently older than the viewership of the TV series." (Nagai, 2006).

mean he doesn't care about her any longer; on the contrary, while Akira's character changes and evolves quite rapidly, he grows even fonder of Miki (and there are many reasons this happens – one being that Miki represents his humanity).

However, in a universe where demons rule, love is anything but easy or straightforward, and Miki is going to become a victim of the second relationship, far more central in Akira's development: the one with Ryo Asuka, otherwise said, Satan.

Plenty has been written on one of the first examples of M/M love in manga/anime aimed to a juvenile public. In 1970s that was probably considered a bit excessive – together with other objectively violent aspects of the manga – and this one of the reasons for Ryo's character disappearance in the 1970s anime[13]; in his place, there is another demon/boy, Himura, Akira's rival for Miki's affection and nothing more. In the original storyline, however, Ryo is so present in Akira's life – his best friend, his soulmate – that Akira's whole transformation happens because he follows Ryo and lets himself be possessed by the great demon Amon[14].

It might be discussed who Ryo/Satan really loves: Akira or Amon. I'd say this is a false problem, because if Ryo selects Akira as Amon's host it is because he has come to love Akira in the first place, and wants to save Akira from the impeding apocalypse to come (the demons are going back to Earth after having inhabited the planet long before humanity); the moment Akira becomes Devilman – a human who can harness Amon's

---

13. Nagai hints at this when declaring "with Ryo, the story developed in surprising ways. The staff of the TV series were rather thrown off by these changes." (Nagai, 2006)

14. In the original manga, this happens thanks to a mask Ryo asks Akira to wear; in the recent anime adaptation *Devilman Crybaby*, it is a techno tune played in a party where demons attack humans after that Ryo challenges them.

power in himself – he is also equipped to survive the return of the demons.

In any case, this is the key relationship in *Devilman*, and Miki doesn't stand a chance[15]; there's no place for her, and she ends up being killed by an angry mob who mistakes her for a witch when the demons scattered across the Earth wreak havoc in her neighbourhood[16].

It is interesting to note that Ryo is not directly involved in the killing of Miki. Of course he's still responsible, because he's the one who exposes Akira as a Devilman to the world, which leads to the persecution and the killing of Miki's family. Still, he doesn't do the deed himself[17] – not because he cares about her, but because she doesn't matter. Ryo doesn't consider her someone who stands in between him and Akira, and it is only when witnessing Akira's reaction to her death that Ryo realises. If there is any jealousy in this triad, it is unidirectional, from Miki for the attentions and the time Akira spends with Ryo.

---

15. Of course, this is not the way the first release of the anime ends, which instead sees Miki and Akira as a happy couple. This was an obliged choice to be able to air the series to an MG audience. The new anime, *Devilman Crybaby*, overall follows the manga into its original, gruesome storyline, albeit simplifying the background story and inserting significant differences in characters, details, and a 21st century setting.

16. A known criticism toward Miki is her lack of agency. This might be because in the original *Devilman* she is not only a character but also a symbol in the manga's complex philosophical universe, in which "her death symbolises the death of peace." (Nagai, 2006). On a different, albeit related point, the treatment of the female protagonist – both in *Devilman* and in *Berserk* –ascribes both series under what Anne Williams defined as one of the distinctive characters of the male Gothic horror compared to a female perspective. "Male Gothic plot and narrative conventions also focus on female suffering, positioning the audience as voyeurs who, though sympathetic, may take pleasure in female victimization," (Williams, 1995, p. 104).

17. This relative indifference of Ryo to Miki and the total lack of interest from Miki's part in Ryo are the reason that makes the relationship in this triad less vicious (and tragic) than in *Berserk*.

Akira's feelings are more complicated. He certainly loves Ryo and he becomes Devilman for him, but it is not romantic love, not of the kind he has for Miki. This aspect becomes more evident toward the end. When Akira founds Miki's head on a spike, he goes stark raving mad[18], first exterminating the angry mob who have executed Miki and then embarking in the final fight against the demons.

The fact it ends badly for him doesn't change the fact that it ends badly for Ryo, too, losing the only one he loves[19]. The manga ends with a crying Ryo, now back into his Satanic (cherubic) form, cradling in his arm the dismembered body of Akira.

In this dark universe, where all main characters either die or end on living miserably, Devilman/Akira is both the most interesting, passing through a series of evolutions and changes, and the most tragic characters –in a Miltonian way.

Ryo/Satan, with his physically ambiguity, that comes from both a long literary tradition (Cazotte,1773; Lewis, 1796, just to mention two examples where the demon can be both male/female in their appearance) and a typical manga trope, and his spectacular beauty[20], remains unaltered in the story,

18. Another detail that will come back in *Berserk*, which starts *in medias res,* with Guts – known as the Black Swordman – in a killing spree mode and on a quest to find and kill demons. The following chapters will show it has been the ordeal of witnessing his woman ravaged by demons (one in particular) that threw Guts in this state.

19. There's a 2000 manga sequel, *Amon*, which Go Nagai co-authored with Yuu Kinutani, telling what remains of Akira when, after his breakdown, his alter-ego demon, Amon, takes over and seeks vengeance. *Amon* ends in a different way from *Devilman*; here Akira/Amon doesn't have his final fight with Ryo/Satan, and just walks away from him, leaving the Devil in deep sorrow.

20. In a well-known trope of Japanese anime and manga, Ryo Asuka is a blond-haired, blue-eyed pretty boy, albeit not androgynous in his original human incarnation (he will become closer to the *bishonen* aesthetics in later instalments). But in his real form, as Satan, is portrayed from the beginning

psychologically speaking, because his power is never really challenged. Only the fact of losing Akira shakes him. He is algid as a remote star[21], and he never openly declares his love to Akira[22].

It is only when he mourns[23] the death of Akira that he shows a profile more 'human', acknowledging the loss and, finally, showing a deeper understanding of the mayhem his actions have brought over – to the world, humans and demons alike, and even to Akira. Demonic love, even when comes from Satan himself, is clearly not enough to save the beloved ones.

The popularity of *Devilman* is immense, and so is its influence on entire generation of mangaka. Its subtropes were going to remain present in the anime/manga tradition, and a more recent manga, *Berserk*, revolves around a similar love

---

as a multi-winged glowing Seraph of an exquisite feminine-like beauty (even a hermaphrodite in the original *Devilman* manga), which reminds closely of Griffith in *Berserk*.

21. In the manga's backstory, Satan originally rebelled against God because "*he was icy*" and did not love his creatures. But this is exactly what Ryo shows to everybody around him, with an exception made for Akira. With that said,, in the manga Ryo/Satan is a character with a strong sense of justice, albeit abstract, and he doesn't show the cynical, at times cruel side that defines him in the animation, both the OVA and *Devilman Crybaby*.

22. It is Satan's most powerful general, Xenon, who makes it plain in the manga in almost mocking terms. "*In this otherwise perfect strategy there has been just one strategic mistake. You have fallen in love with the human Akira Fudo. You've done anything you could possibly do to let Akira live among the demons, even sacrificing the great Amon,*" [Vol. 3, Episode 2]. In *Devilman Crybaby*, these feelings are a bit more explicit – when weeping over Akira's lifeless body in his arms, Ryo openly say that now he understands what love is because of Akira – but still on a restrained note compared to, say, *Berserk*.

23. This might be due to the way Satan has been condemned to suffer for his rebellion. In an unexpected twist of pessimism and cosmic cruelty, it comes out in the manga sequel *Amon* that God has put the universe in a sort of existence cycle to punish Satan and make him live again and again the loss of his beloved.

triangle of two men and a woman, but with even darker tones and a truly gruesome twist, as it will be shown in section 5. In *Berserk*, love and desire themselves are portrayed "as fascinating, enslaving, destroying the self" and therefore "to be considered for definition as demonic" (Testa, 1991, p.3) and leading people in love straight to their downfall. And if one wonders what happens when Lucifer's heart truly breaks, Miura has provided quite a convincing answer.

Versailles no bara (*Lady Oscar*): broken hearts and *amour de loin*

Riyoko Ikeda's *Versailles no Bara* [ベルサイユのばら] (1972-73) is one of the most famous *shojo* manga of all times, currently ranked 14th on the list of all-time bestselling shōjo, with about 15 million volumes worldwide sales, 12 million in Ikeda's home country. The anime adaptation became so successful overseas and contributed so much to the popularity of the French culture[24] in Japan that Ikeda was awarded the France's highest honour – *Ordre national de la Légion d'honneur* (National Order of the Legion of Honour) – in 2009[25].

The attractiveness of a character like Oscar Francois de

---

24. And history as well. *Versailles no Bara*, apart from the obvious fictional characters, is startling accurate, including many (largely unknown) details, including the accusations of lesbianism against Marie Antoinette, the Affair of the Necklace, and supporting characters (Jeanne Valois). Others are inspired to historical people, albeit fictionalised, such as Rosalie Lamoriel (one of Marie Antoinette's servants in the revolutionary jail of La Conciergerie) and Bernard Chatelet, probably inspired by the journalist Desmoulins.

25. Read the story at: <https://www.animenewsnetwork.com/news/2009-03-12/rose-of-versailles-ikeda-receives-france-top-honor>. The number of Japanese tourists who visit Le Petit Trianon, the famous palace of Marie Antoinette, is second in France only to national visitors (Marrion Barron, 2018).

Jarjayes, the youngest daughter of a general, who, for lack of male issue, decides to raise her a man, is easy to understand in terms of feminism and female empowerment, and not only in Japan. More interesting is the innovative spin of given by Ikeda to her main character (as discussed by Duggan, 2013). Maiden warriors were a staple both in classical Chinese literature (Hua Mulan) and French traditions (Jeanne d'Arc), but all of them fought as men for a patriarchal, male-led system, defending the established values. Oscar allies herself with the revolutionaries, dying as a hero at the Bastille in 14 July 1789.

Interesting as well is the analysis of the subject of love in *Versailles no Bara*, under many aspects[26]. First of all, this is probably where unrequited love in Japanese manga and anime reaches one of its most tragic incarnations.

None of the four main characters (Oscar, Queen Marie Antoinette, Count Hans-Axel of Fersen and Andre' Grendier, Oscar's childhood companion and servant)[27], for one reason or another, can be together with the person they love.

Fersen and Maria Antoinette love each other but, apart for a brief spell of a furtive dalliance, they must be parted, suffering their separation and loving each other from afar, in the most typical Jaufre Rudel-like impossible love[28] of the

---

26. Since the anime are more well known outside Japan than the manga, all quotes here comes from the anime episodes.

27. The unrequited love is not confined to them, though. Others go through this as well, falling in love for Oscar without being corresponded, such as Comte Girodel, Oscar's second in command in the Royal Guard, and, in the manga at least (in the anime this detail is left out) Alain de Saisson, a man in the National Guard who will become Oscar and Andre's good friend. Alain is also the protagonist of Lady Oscar's sequel, *Eikou no Napoleon* [栄光のナポ レオン－エロイカ], *The glory of Napoleon* or *Eroica*, which follows instead the life of Napoleon from the aftermath of the French revolution, his rise to power and eventual demise.

28. Jaufre Rudel's famous poem *No sap chantar qui so non di*, echoes in his stanzas this kind of feelings. See, for instance, stanza #5 '*A faraway love kills*

Provençal tradition that so fascinated Romantic poets in the 19th century, Heinrich Heine, Algernon Charles Swinburne, Robert Browning and Giosue Carducci among them.

But Fersen and the Queen[29] are not the only ones who suffer.

Oscar, too, loves Fersen in silence, and only betrays herself when, for the first and only time in her life, she dresses as a woman to dance with him and find out his true feelings (only friendship) for her[30]. As Fersen is blind to Oscar's feelings for him, Oscar is blind about her long-time friend Andre', who declares himself in despair only when Oscar tells him that she wants to live as a true man and does not need his assistance any longer.

It is in Andre's words that Ikeda expresses the concept of love from afar, Japanese style, in two specific episodes

The first is in Episode 20, when, talking about Fersen's forbidden affair with the Queen, Andre's declares "*I have the impression this great love gives him more pain than happiness. There are people who love others all their life without their love interests even realise it,*" to which Oscar doesn't say a word (not realising Andre was talking about himself and instead thinking about her own unrequited feelings towards Fersen).

The other is Andre's internal monologue, when Oscar decides to renounce the command of the Royal Guard. "*Why do you want to quit the Royal Guard? Having said farewell to Fersen, you want to flee from Marie Antoinette whom Fersen*

---

me /and the sweet longing stands by me /and when I plan on going there/ my will remains here/I don't escape my death, which won't be otherwise.' (Rudel, sd, online).

29. In the anime, Fersen's suffering gets more coverage, due also to his role as the object of Oscar's unrequired love. In the manga, however, Marie Antoinette's own sorrow is clearly expressed in the last moments of her life, when she is in front of the guillotine and her last thoughts are all for Fersen.

30. In Episode 25, while dancing with her (without knowing her true identity) he calls her "his most precious and beautiful friend".

loves? If leaving were the solution, I would have left you many years ago. It's useless to run away, Oscar. Believe me" [Episode 28].

But there is nowhere as in the fateful exchange between Fersen and Oscar that the expression of unrequited love is more profound. Challenged by Fersen about her own feelings for him, Oscar cries "*love can lead to two things: to a complete happiness or to a slow and sad agony*". Fersen, in tears as well, answers back, "*no, Oscar. For what I know, love only leads to a slow, sad agony*" [Episode 28].

The relationship between Oscar and Andre', which finally ends in a reciprocated love before they both die the day after during the onset of the revolution, has been discussed a lot in literature for the influence it carried on successive *shojo* manga.

Suzuki (1999) noticed the discovery of 'womanliness' by formerly asexual girls due to love[31], which was replicated further on. Shamoon (2007) singles out their relationship as distinctively different from the typical Prince Charming-style stories which "dominated" *shōjo* manga in the 1960s and 1970s, where the female protagonist would become submissive of her boyfriend. Oscar and André's relationship is instead a relationship among equals, which, rather following the pattern of the Meiji era *dōseiai* (同性愛, same sex/gender) love novels, featuring same-sex love between girls, is romantic more than sexual.

Others, such as Thompson (2017), go further and classify

---

31. This detail also became recurrent outside the *shojo* audience. An example is another 1980 anime, a mecha *shonen, Baldios*. Here the main antagonist is Aphrodia, the Commander in Chief of the enemy armies, who, by her own admission "has renounced to be a woman the day her brother Miran has been killed" (Ep. 25 "The Conspiracy"). The fact that her brother's killer is Marin Rigel, Baldios's main pilot and later in the story, Aphrodia's love interest, creates her many identity issues and the painful realisation she's a woman (in love).

Versailles no Bara as a *yuri* manga, specifically devoted to exploring sexual and romantic relationships among women, and consider it, therefore, precious in the context of queer studies. In her analysis of the Palace of Versailles, Thomson says that 'the Rose of Versailles creates queer rhetorical places that challenge traditional histories of the French Revolution and that enable queer viewers to reorient and extend their bodies into fantastical visual spaces of eighteenth-century France' (Thompson, 2017, p.306).

It is fair to say that, more than outwardly queer, Versailles no Bara is genderfluid, with the main character dressed and living as a man all her life, even though the line is often blurred. The queer component is left rather subdued in the anime's 40 episodes, in spite of a few references, and it is only in the relationship of Oscar and Rosalie Lamoriel that this component of same-sex love becomes more apparent (see Episode 17, where Rosalie makes a passing reference to her 'great love for Oscar' when acknowledging her jealousy toward the Queen Marie Antoinette). On the other hand, queer references and narrative subtext are more explicit in the manga[32].

What stays common to both versions is Oscar herself, with her dazzling, at times aloof but always charismatic personality, fancied and admired by both women and men and that well represents the conventional *shojo* manga depiction of Western attractiveness (Napier, 1998). She is the sort of perfect ideal of a slender, blonde-haired, blue-eyed beauty present in both *Devilman* and *Berserk*. But where Ryo and Griffith show the demonic side of the model, Oscar is like an archangel, living as a truly moral character and dying like a hero. Beauty *can* be good.

---

32. In the manga, Rosalie openly declares Oscar to be her first love.

Everybody hurts. Fall from grace, madness, and revenge in *Berserk*[33]

The last series analysed here is Kentaro Miura's *Berserk* [ベルセルク] (1989-present), a *seinen* manga directly related to both *Devilman* – for obvious reasons – and, more surprisingly to *Versailles no Bara*, which Miura himself credited as one of his main sources of inspiration[34].

Millions of words have been written about *Berserk*, often called 'the *Game of Thrones* of the manga universe[35]' (albeit Miura started publishing it well before *GoT*). Almost in no other manga there is such a complex, multilayered, philosophical-heavy universe like in this creation serialised as a manga since 1990 in 40 volumes (and counting), combining a plethora of different inspirations and cultural inputs and different genres, SF, fantasy and horror among them.

While Miura looked at *Versailles no Bara* for the intrigue-heavy representation of the court of Midland, the world he portrays is as dark and violent as *Devilman*. And if there's a manga that shows how destructive love can possibly be, it is *Berserk*.

As in Go Nagai's creation, we have a triad[36].

---

33. [Content warning: *Berserk* is possibly the darkest offering in the manga universe. It covers disturbing topics and portrays even more disturbing scenes, including mass murder and rape. While this article won't look at them in detail, it will still reference them when necessary for the analysis undertaken here.]

34. He allegedly declared *Berserk* as the result of his attempt to fuse the worlds of *Fist of the North Star* and *Versailles no Bara*. See Miura (1996).

35. See, for instance, Vanderpoort (2019).

36. Due to the article's focus, the analysis concentrates on Griffith, a sort of medieval incarnation of Lucifer, "full of wisdom and perfect in beauty", and follows his trajectory through his downfall and his resurrection as a Satan-like demon, Femto. It therefore leaves out Guts and Casca's own

An angelic-looking character of the Ryo Asuka type, Griffith, seductive and proud as Lucifer[37] before the Fall and who aims at creating a kingdom for himself; Guts, a mercenary, dark and sulky like Akira post-demonic transformation, who's enlisted at a certain moment in Griffith's army, the Band of the Hawk; and Casca, Griffith's second-in-command, another warrior maiden in male clothing like Oscar but without her personality and revolutionary *élan*[38].

In this case, the triangle is complicated by the fact that Casca, before becoming Guts's love interest, is besotted with Griffith and jealous of the attentions her idol reserves for Guts[39]. It is only when she understands that Griffith is outside her reach that she shifts her interest to Guts, just when Guts itself decides

motivations, fatal mistakes/miscalculations, and character arcs. They're both tragic protagonists: Guts, because has suffered everything a man can possibly suffer, and the only woman he eventually manages to care about, Casca, is taken from him in a truly awful way. Casca's destiny is even worse. She lacks Oscar's self-confidence and perception of her value, and the moment she starts outgrowing her psychological dependence from Griffith and finds someone who can appreciate her for what she is, she becomes collateral damage of the love-hate dynamics between the two men of her life. In *Berserk*, everybody truly hurts.

37. All the symbolism about Griffith, the white Hack of Light (always in his white armour with a helmet like a Hawk), recalls an angel, and so it is his fall from heaven that turns him into a demon, the 'Wing of Darkness'.

38. Unlike *Versailles No Bara*, here it is not Casca but Griffith who takes Oscar's angelic long blond hair, blue eyes, and androgynous look. Like Oscar, Griffith's exquisite beauty and charm attract like a magnet both men and women. Unlike Oscar, he has narcissistic traits and uses his charm to achieve his objectives.

39. Differently from *Devilman*, here the queer subtext is much more explicit, both in terms of wording and imagery. Griffith addresses Guts with phrases such as "you are mine"; "I want you"; "if I can't have you (nobody will)". The proof it is not something anodyne comes from Guts himself, who, during their first encounter, replies startled "*are you a Homo?*", and, before their first fight,"*[If you win] then you make me your soldier or fag boy or whatever,*" [Volume 4, Episode 12, "Golden Age-5"].

at the same moment to leave Griffith's army – *and* Griffith – and go his own way.

It doesn't take a genius to imagine this would end badly, but nobody imagined just how bad it would turn out to be. Saying Miura shocked the manga world is an understatement.

Guts's departure destroys Griffith, but the degree of his despair is not initially apparent to anybody, not even Griffith himself[40]. On a dangerous gamble, he seduces Princess Charlotte, whom he had already envisaged marrying for political reasons. Charlotte's father, the Midland King, finds out and punishes Griffith by throwing him in jail and torturing him for an entire year. When Guts and Casca eventually rescue him, Griffith is a shadow of his former self, physically a wreck and borderline sane. But not insane, as people in the fandom have something claimed: everything Griffith does afterwards is sane, albeit morally reproachable until it becomes vicious.

This is the moment when readers start getting a heads-up about nastier things to come: the first thing Griffith does when Guts opens the jail and comes to his help is not to embrace him[41] in gratitude, but to strangle him; he stops only when he

---

40. Griffith's excellent capabilities at compartmentalisation, which have served him well in his rise to political power, here prove to be his downfall. He only realises it after a long year of tortures, seeing his feelings clearly for the first time. "*Darkness. Deep darkness without even a trace of light. How much time has passed since I was cast into this darkness...? [...] In all this emptiness...only one thing is vivid. Only him. Like lightning on a dark night, he rises up within me, blazing. And again and again like a tidal wave, an infinite number of feelings surge upon me. [...] I have grasped the hearts of so many in these hands. But why is it when it comes to him, I always lose my composure? He was the reason I've been thrown into the darkness, and now he's the sole sustenance keeping me alive*" [Volume 10, Episode 49, "Infiltrating Windham"].

41. At least in terms of attempts: Griffith can't say anything because his tongue has been pulled out, nor he can move a great deal, as his tendons of wrists and ankles have been severed.

sees Guts crying. He lets go of his anger and resentment and abandons himself in Guts's arms. Moreover, after catching Guts and Casca in a sweet moment, his first reaction is an attempt to have sex with Casca (only wishful thinking, of course, considering his present condition). There are two alternative interpretations usually put forward for Griffith's strange behaviour with her[42], but they're both influenced by what happens next; Griffith is not psychologically there yet. There is another, more convincing explanation: Griffith wants to have sex with Casca because she's now Guts's woman. This is a well-known mechanism anthropologists have extensively written about, both at a sociological level – marrying the woman of another clan is the way to create alliances (Levy-Strauss, 1967) – and a more intimate level, with the objectification of the feminine body as an instrument to put males in relation with each other (Magli, 1987)[43].

Whatever the motive, this represents one of Griffith's last, albeit flawed, acts of humanity. Lucifer has fallen from grace the moment Guts has left, but it is only now that he sees his broken wings and his Paradise Lost, which leads straight to tragedy.

---

42. According to a common opinion in the fandom, he wants to force himself on her because in his eyes Casca is guilty twice: she has betrayed him (Casca was his Lieutenant, but also one of the few he was close to, albeit not friends with) and, worse, she has taken Guts for herself (and Guts is willing to remain within the Band of Hawk for her while he has previously abandoned Griffith). Another view is that he tries to reassert the psychological dominance he had over her. Neither are correct: Casca has never mattered to him in a romantic way, and she doesn't matter now. The only thing different here is that she is now Guts's lover.

43. "*[L'incontro e] lo scontro fra potenze maschili avviene, dunque, tramite la femminilità.*" (Magli, 1987, p. 134). This is not even the first time Casca serves in this role. After his first fight with Guts, Griffith orders Casca to sleep near a wounded Guts to warm him up and help him heal faster (as this is "*the role of a woman*") even though she has renounced to live as a woman to serve as a swordsman.

Griffith at this point does the only thing he can do[44]: he invokes the Eclipse[45], where, in a series of bloodcurdling tableaux of hordes of demons and mass sacrifices (with visual references to Gustave Dore', *Alien*'s creator H. R. Giger, and Hieronymus Bosch among them), he gives up everything he cares about to turn himself into a real demon[46], Femto[47], one of the God's Hand.

Griffith's last words before the ultimate sacrifice remind closely of Roland Barthes's *A Lover's Discourse*'s famous quote[48] and settle forever the debate whether Griffith loves Guts in a romantic way: "*among thousands of comrades and ten thousand enemies, you're the only one. The only one who made me forget my dream,*" [Volume 12, Episode 78, "Parting"].

A lot has been written about the gruesome pages of *Berserk*'s Volume 13, Episodes #86-87, where Griffith/Femto rapes Casca in front of Guts and forces him to watch. What remains the most in the readers' memory is not the violence of

---

44. Not before trying to kill himself first, showing that what comes next was neither inevitable nor an act of premeditated evil on his part. Griffith becomes absolute evil as a consequence of a series of ill-fated choices and events, damned both by his love for Guts and his incapability of acknowledging it.

45. I won't go into details for reasons of space here, but even the modalities of the sacrifice itself are meaningful, because to make it happen, Griffith has to renounce what is most precious to him.

46. Torture as the key motivation in becoming a demon and 'embracing darkness' is a well-known theme in manga/anime. See, for instance, *Tokyo Ghouls*, where Kaneki accepts to become a ghoul only after being tortured.

47. Symbolic analysis is outside the scope of this article, but the use of the colour purple in Femto's depiction in the anime (and movie adaptation) and the entire concept of *hanshin* (transformation, demonic and not), so popular in the anime and manga culture (Gill, 1998) are to be noted.

48. "I encounter millions of bodies in my life; of these millions, I may desire some hundreds; but of these hundreds, I love only one," (Barthes, 1977, p. 45).

the Eclipse[49] but the duel of stares between Guts and Griffith, which foreshadows both the sequel and the leitmotif of the whole manga.

Those pages are not about lust – they're anything but lust. Griffith doesn't care about sex with Casca, as much as he didn't care about Princess Charlotte. If anything, Griffith is almost asexual, and every time we see him involved in sex acts the motivation lies elsewhere than in desire, starting from when he prostitutes himself to Lord Gennon to gather the money necessary for the cause. The closest he gets to acting on an impulse sex-wise is with Charlotte after Guts abandons him in what looks like a (unsuccessful) mechanism to cope with the loss[50]. However, those pages are not about vengeance either. Certainly Griffith wants to make Guts suffer, but if vengeance were the only reason, he would kill Casca (without or after ravaging her). What Griffith aims at doing are two things, which might look theoretically opposite but are very much in line with the way human emotions work. The first is to prove to himself his 'heart is frozen'; he's now reborn as pure evil, and he doesn't care any longer about Guts. He can nail him where it hurts the most: the woman Guts cares about[51].

Second and most important, he ties Guts forever to him; having failed with love, he does it through hatred[52], leaving

---

49. The prelude is the massacre of the Band of the Hawk itself as the required sacrifice for Femto to be born; also, Guts severs his own arm to try to free himself from the demons who are holding him and rescue Casca.

50. Therefore, the often-asked question if he loves Guts in a sexual way is irrelevant.

51. I won't even enter the discussion about who is Guts' *true* love interest, because it would require a different analysis. I am personally persuaded it is, and always be, Griffith, which is what makes *Berserk* so tragic. What is not a matter of contention is that Guts *does* care about Casca, and the Eclipse devastates him.

52. Nobody better than Jeanette Winterson explained the twin emotions of

Guts with a deeply traumatised companion[53] (and making the unborn son of Guts and Casca a misshapen demon-child[54], as if the rest was not enough), like a daily reminder and pain that never goes away. Guts will never forget, will never let go, and will remain in the mental prison Griffith has thrown him in during the Eclipse. For the rest of his days – and the still-ongoing manga – Guts will leave a trail of blood and dead bodies in his quest to find Griffith/Femto and get even, and nothing else will really matter.

The Miltonian ritual of the most beautiful among the angels falling from paradise to be reborn as a cruel-beyond-cruelty demon is now complete.

Conclusions

Japanese manga and anime present a series of complex universes, full of cultural references and a mix of genres, often tackling crucial philosophical and ontological subjects. Love is one of them, and nowhere is it seen as strongly as in the trope of unrequited love: it is here that this depth becomes

---

love and hatred. "I didn't know what hate felt like, not the hate that comes after love. It's huge and desperate and it longs to be proved wrong. And every day it's proved right it grows a little more monstrous. If the love was passion, the hate will be obsession. A need to see the once-loved weak and cowed beneath pity." (Winterson, 1987, p. 120). This could well describe not only Guts's all-consuming rage against Griffith after the Eclipse, but also Griffith/Femto's attitude toward Guts when they first meet again. "*Still squirming into your pitiful existence, are you?*" [Volume 1, Episode 3].

53. She loses her memory, regresses in a childlike traumatised state, and rejects Guts.

54. *Berserk* is a manga full of symbolism and philosophical and literary references, which were not examined in this article for reasons of space. It is only the case to notice that the demon-baby serves here both as a symbol (Huet, 1993; Kristeva, 1980) and as a plot device.

apparent in all its nuances and implications. From a way to assert feminist equality in a relationship while crying for love from afar (*Versailles no Bara*) to destructive passions that overwhelm the self (*Berserk*) or a cosmic way of expiating a capital sin (*Devilman*), unrequited love Japanese style is a unique, emotional, and compelling creation.

Bibliography

Barthes, R., 1977. *A lover's discourse: fragments*; Translation edition (October 12, 2010). New York: Hill and Wang.

Berserk [ベルセルク], Miura, K., *Monthly Animal House* since 1989. English Publisher: Dark Horse Manga October 1989 – present. 40 volumes (ongoing).

Cazotte, J., 1776. *Le Diable Amoureux* (trad: The Devil in Love 1993). New York: Marsilio.

Devilman [デビルマン] Nagai, G., *Kodansha*, June 11, 1972 - June 24, 1973. English Publisher: Seven Seas Entertainment (5 volumes).

Duggan, A.E., 2013. The Revolutionary Undoing of the Maiden Warrior in Riyoko Ikeda's *Rose of Versailles* and Jacques Demy's *Lady Oscar*. *Marvels & Tales* 27.1. Available at: <https://digitalcommons.wayne.edu/marvels/vol27/iss1/2> [Accessed 15 December 2019].

Gill, T., 1998. Transformational Magic. In D. Martinez (Ed.), *The Worlds of Japanese Popular Culture: Gender, Shifting Boundaries and Global Cultures in Contemporary Japanese Society*, 33-55. Cambridge: Cambridge University Press.

Huet, M., 1993. *Monstrous Imagination*. Cambridge (MA) & London: Harvard University Press.

Kristeva, J., 1980. *Powers of Horror: An Essay on Abjection*, New York: Columbia University Press.

Lacan, J., 1966. *The Subversion of the Subject and the Dialectic of Desire in the Freudian Unconscious.*

Lewis, M., 1796/1983. *The Monk*. Ed. Howard Anderson. Oxford & NY: Oxford University Press.

Magli I., 1987. *La Madonna*, Milano: Rizzoli

Maior-Barron, D., 2018. *Marie Antoinette at Petit Trianon: Heritage Interpretation and Visitor*. London: Routledge.

Miura, K., 1996. Interview with Kentaro Miura. *Berserk Illustrations File*, (1996-12-04) on Berserk Wiki Fandom website. Available at: <https://berserk.fandom.com/wiki/Interviews>. [Accessed 15 December 2019].

Nagai, G., 2006. Devilman Revelations. *Kodansha*. Available at: <http://devilworld.org/revelations.html>. [Accessed 15 December 2019].

Napier, S.J., 1998. Vampires, Psychic Girls, Flying Women and Sailor Scouts. In Martinez, D.P. (ed.). *The Worlds of Japanese Popular Culture: Gender, Shifting Boundaries and Global Culture*. Cambridge University Press.

Raudel, J., ed. *Complete works*. Available at: <http://www.trobar.org/troubadours/jaufre_rudel/> [Accessed 15 December 2019].

Shamoon, D., 2007. Revolutionary Romance: The Rose of Versailles and the Transformation of Shōjo Manga. In Lunning, F., ed.. *Networks of Desire*. Mechademia. 2. University of Minnesota Press Perceptions, London: Routledge.

Shamoon, D., 2009. The Second Coming of Shôjo. *Heso Magazine*. Available at: <https://hesomagazine.com/japan/the-second-coming-of-shojo/>. [Accessed 15 December 2019].

Levy-Strauss, C., 1949/1969. *Les Structures élémentaires de la parenté. The Elementary Structures of Kinship*. Boston: Bacon Press

Suzuki, K., 1999. Pornography or Therapy? Japanese Girls Creating the Yaoi Phenomenon. In Inness, S. ed., *Millennium Girls: Today's Girls Around the World*. London: Rowman & Littlefield.

Testa, C., 1990 *Desire and the Devil*. Available at: < https://www.academia.edu/19832816/TESTA_C_-_DESIRE_AND_THE_DEVIL>. [Accessed 15 December 2019].

Suvilay B., 2017. Neon Genesis Evangelion ou la déconstruction du robot anime. *Revue d'études sur la science-fiction*, (7)1-16. Available at: <http://resf.revues.org/954>. [Accessed 15 December 2019].

Thompson, K.D., 2017. The Cross-Cultural Power of Yuri: Riyoko Ikeda's Queer Rhetorics of Place-Making in *The Rose of Versailles*. *Peitho* 19.2, pp.301-20.

Vanderpoort N., 2019. 5 Ways Berserk and Game of Thrones Are Similar (& 5 Ways They Aren't). 11 July, *CBR.com.* Available at: <https://www.cbr.com/ berserk-game-thrones-similarities-differences> [Accessed 15 December 2019].

Versailles No Bara [ベルサイユのばら] Ikeda, R., *Shueisha*, May 1972 – December 1973. English Publisher: Udon Entertainment (13 volumes)

Williams, A., 1995. *Art of Darkness. A Poetics of Gothic*, Chicago: University of Chicago Press.
Winterson, J., 1987. *The Passion*. London: Bloomsbery.

List of Manga / Anime referenced in this article

Amon
Attack on Titan
Baldios
Berserk
Char's Counterattack [OVA belonging to the Gundam franchise]
Mao Dante
Devilman
Devilman Crybaby
Eroica [The glory of Napoleon]
Gundam -Mobil Suit 1979
Gundam - Ironblood Orphans
Gundam Z
Gundam ZZ
Gundam Victory
Gundam Wings
Neon Genesis Evangelion
Okuto-no-Ken [Fist of the North Star]
Saint-Seiya
Tokyo Ghouls
Versailles no Bara

Tragic Lovers: Fated or Chosen?
A Critical Analysis of *An Orchestra of Minorities* by Chigozie Obioma and *The Concubine* by Elechi Amadi in the Light of Igbo Metaphysics

Ezeiyoke Chukwunonso

Abstract

Speculative literature is full of tragic lovers. In Greek mythology, we read about Orpheus and Eurydice. Orpheus, whose wife died on their wedding night, travelled to the underworld to rescue her. Alas, his triumphant story of rescuing her from Hades ended tragically when he failed the bailing condition Hades gave him. The doomed love between Winston and Julia, in George Orwell's *1984*, was of a different nature. It showed how one's humanity could erode little by little when subjected to tortuous tyranny. And it raises the question of which one succeeds: love or self-preservation? *The Concubine* by Amadi followed a similar path to Orpheus and Eurydice, of men trying to save a doomed love. *An Orchestra of Minorities*, by Obioma however, was different. It followed the story of a man who falls in love with a woman who later falls out of love with him; the man by then had become obsessed with her, and that was a recipe for disaster. But there is a close link between the tragic love in *Concubine* and that in the *Orchestra of Minorities*, in the sense that both lovers were doomed to tragic ends by circumstances surrounding them and by mechanisms beyond their control. These two novels raise a pertinent question: do lovers who think themselves in charge of the direction of their love really have a choice, or are they either doomed or fated for blissfulness by sheer forces beyond them?

This essay, while exploring the worldview and the cosmology

found in Igbo Metaphysics upon which the novels were based, will critically examine the roles of freedom and determinism in regard to who, and how, one gets bonded to as a lover, even when the road is a tragic one.

Introduction

> Guardian spirits of mankind, have we thought about the powers that passion creates in a human being? Have we considered why a man could run through a field of fire to get to a woman he loves? (Obioma 2019, pp.59-60)

It is often taken for granted that in relationships couples are together out of free will or choice. If this is removed, the essential ingredient of the union is missing. Without freedom, what is left is no longer love but bondage because, in love, one freely gives oneself to their beloved. Giving presupposes being free, because one can only give what they are able to choose to either withhold or hand out. A Latin adage articulated it thus: *nemo dat quod non habet* (no one gives what they don't have). The marriage oath captured this essence of liberty among lovers.

But what if, by a certain design, the couple taking this oath and thinking that they were acting freely were not? That their relationship was in fact preordained beforehand? That their actions followed a path predetermined by a mechanism beyond them, as if they were characters in a book authored by someone else? Obioma put it thus: "I have come to understand that the things that happen to a man have already occurred long before in some subterranean realm, and that nothing in the universe is without precedent." (Obioma, 2019, p.26)"

Obioma's assertion may sound like supernatural metaphysics but the whole point of causality, cause and effect, is that action is equal to reaction, and the physical sciences are built upon this, as Newton's third law of motion declares. Therefore, for any reaction one sees, there has been an equal and opposite action. And if we concur with the above assertion, that everything that happens to a man (reaction) has already had a precedent (action), love included, then couples are bonded either to doom or success in their love life, since their love life (reaction) necessarily proceeded from an already occurred event (action).

This assertion is problematic, though. What it set up is an ancient philosophical argument between freedom and determinism that had confronted thinkers throughout the history of philosophy for quite some time. What Chigozie Obioma and Elechi Amadi did in their respective novels, *An Orchestra of Minorities* (2019) and *The Concubine* (1966), is to confront this ambiguity by paying credence to Igbo Metaphysics. With their narratives, they tried to give different philosophical answers to the problem of fatalism and choice that occurs when one is bonded by love.

In this essay, we will examine how these novels demonstrated this and whether they succeeded in their ambitions.

Igbo Metaphysics

Igbo Metaphysics can be found within the general discussion of Metaphysics and African philosophy. E.M.P. Edeh, a pioneer scholar in Igbo Metaphysics, began his enquiry in response to the same question that led to the emergence of African philosophy as a whole: does Africa have a philosophy? This question is an urgent one because it touches on the core humanness of an African person. If Africans do not have a philosophy, it implies that they do not have a systematic process of reasoning, and those without methodological reasoning are subhuman in light of Hegel's thought. We will soon see how he denied Africans 'the Knowledge of an absolute Being' (Hegel, 1884, p.97). In this light, you can understand why Outlaw summed up the origin of African philosophy thus:

> ... the twentieth-century emergence of African philosophy [...] work with a distinctive mission: to gather up and explore critically thoughtful articulations and aesthetic expressions by and about persons and peoples African and of African descent [...] and to fashion revised or new articulations and artful expressions in keeping with, and as aids to, quests for freedom, justice, and human dignity by and for these persons and peoples. (Outlaw, 2017)

This is their quest; to restore African human dignity which had been blown to pieces by the racial philosophy of people like Hegel, who said:

> The African in the uniform, undeveloped oneness of his existence has not yet attained; so that the Knowledge of an absolute Being, an Other and a Higher than his individual self, is entirely wanting. The Negro, as already observed, exhibits the natural man in his completely wild and untamed state. We must lay aside all thought of reverence and morality—all that we call feeling—if we would rightly comprehend him; there is nothing harmonious with humanity to be found in this type of character. (Hegel, 1884, p.97)

or Kant, who corroborated Hegel's racial bias when, in his book *Observations of the Beautiful and the Sublime*, quoted by Yancy, he said,

The Negroes of Africa have by nature no feeling that rises above the trifling. Mr. Hume challenges anyone to cite a single example in which a Negro has shown talents, and asserts that among the hundreds of thousands of blacks who are transported elsewhere from their countries, although many of them have even been set free, still not a single one was ever found who presented anything great in art or science or any other praiseworthy quality. (Kant in Yancy, 2004, p.147)

That made Edeh, Okere (who began Hermeneutic trends in African philosophy) and other African philosophers, turn to the traditional thought process of the African community, extracting its philosophical concepts and placing it on a par with Western thought. This was done to show that a systematic thought pattern similar to that of the West could be located in Africa, albeit with some notable differences between the two. The emphasis here was that each thought-process was methodological. From this starting point, those philosophers began their own philosophical enterprise. This mode of enquiry went back to Tempels, who 'set out to help European missionaries understand the thought pattern or worldview of the Bantu people' (Kanu, 2018, p.12). An unintended consequence of this is that it oriented African philosophy to enable it to become a field whose gaze looked outward.

Metaphysics, as a noun, is a branch of philosophy derived from the Greek phrase "meta ta physika", meaning "After physics". Okpala articulated the origin of the discipline thus:

Metaphysics is the name Andronicus of Rhodes gave Aristotle's books [...]. Metaphysics for Aristotle is the study of being as being; it is the final degree of abstraction, where things could be conceived independently of matter. (Okpala, 2002, p.559)

However, the search of what lay behind its appearance did not start with Aristotle. When the earlier Ionian philosophers were searching for the basic elements and proposed Earth, Air, Fire, Water, they were in fact searching for the foundation behind the transit appearance they witnessed every day; they were searching for the being *qua* being of every existence; the unchanged behind every change.

Over time, schools of thought emerged to account for this phenomenon. Plato argued that physical reality participates in the non-physical. Aristotle insisted that the non-physical causes the physical. (Okpala, 2002)

In Igbo Metaphysics, this idea of the non-physical causing the physical is articulated with the idiom, "ihe kwuru ihe akwudube ya", because for every physical appearance, there is a known physical cause behind it (Okpala, 2002); or, as Edeh put it, "ife ya na ya yi" (Ede, 1985, p.79). Okpala noted that 'Igbo metaphysics does not dissociate "being" from "knowing," nor does it isolate "knowing" from "being" and "acting." Igbo metaphysics is a "thought- system which recognizes the reality and independent existence" of non-physical beings and their interaction with physical beings in the material world' (Okpala, 2002, p.557).

Now let us turn back to Obioma and Elechi's novels and examine how they used Igbo metaphysics in their bid to answer the question of fatalism and choice in relationships.

Love in *An Orchestra of Minorities*: Fated or Chosen

The novel opens with *Chi*, a guardian spirit and narrator of the novel, in front of God to intercede for its host.

Obasidinelu, I stand before you [...] like other guardian spirits,

I have gone to uwa in many cycles of reincarnations, inhabiting a freshly created body each time (Obioma, 2019, p.1).

There is an urgency in this plea because the host Chinonso has committed manslaughter by killing Ndali, the woman he loves but who has fallen out of love with him. Even though her death was an accident, it becomes irrelevant because Ndali was pregnant at the time. Ala, the goddess of land and fertility, will certainly take revenge. Chinonso being alive is just a mere biding of his time. His death is already sealed.

The ill luck that has befallen a man has long been waiting for him […] but in truth the man had died long ago, the reality of his death merely concealed by a silken veil of time, which would eventually be parted to reveal it (p.27).

Edeh, noting Igbo justice relating to murder, said:

Among the Igbos, murder is the most serious sin. Murder, whether accidentally or intentionally committed, is regarded as murder insofar as life is lost. [...] Even today in Igboland if you, while driving, knock somebody down dead, the people around the scene must make sure that they kill you on the spot (Edeh, 1985, p.37).

Given the severity of murder (accidental or not), *Chi* knows that there is no point in interceding with Chukwu for Chinonso's life to be spared. Despite this, *Chi* says to Chukwu, in defence of Chinonso, "Egbunu, how could he have thought that a woman who had a house would choose to sleep at her place of work? No. Why would she? There was no reason for him to think so" (Obioma, 2019, p.511). What *Chi* seeks is for Chinonso to be admitted to the domains of Alamuo, in the company of his forefathers, so that the cycle of his life can continue. This is because life is nothing but a carnival, consisting of coming and going. Achebe noted that 'spirit land […] recreate a life comparable to their earthly existence is not only parallel to the human world but is also similar and physically contiguous with it for there is constant coming and going between them in the endless traffic of life, death and reincarnation' (Achebe, 1998, p.68). But there could be a disruption to this party, to this travelogue called existence. The real tragedy is when the cycle breaks. Crime brings forth this breakage. And that is exactly where Chinonso has landed himself. Depending on the judgement of Chukwu, the supreme being, Chinonso could end up being an akaliogili, a vagabond spirit desperately searching for a human body to unite with. In others words, damnation.

Looking at this, one could think that the whole set-up in the novel is about freedom and choice. Chinonso freely chooses not to move on when the woman he loves leaves him. In anger, because of how she treated him, he burns her shop down, unaware that she's sleeping inside.

As Chinonso chooses revenge, the consequences of his actions are deserved. His anger destroys him. Being an akoligoli is the potential punishment waiting for him because of his choice.

On the surface, one could assume that Chinonso has made his choice and he is about to face the consequences. In this sense, fatalism has played no role in the love between him and Ndali, a love that has turned tragic and has ended in death.

However, when one considers the role of nonphysical circumstances beyond the physical manifestation, that being Chinonso, the whole perspective on his action does change.

In Igbo cosmology, the narrator of the novel, *Chi*, the

guardian spirit, is not just a mere angel whose role is to guide or to testify on behalf of his host to Chukwu. *Chi* embodies the spiritual significance of the physical manifestation. *Chi* is in fact the spiritual manifestation of human existence. It is the "ife kwuru ife akwubedoya" of human existence (Edeh, 1985, p.77). Achebe described *Chi* thus: 'The world in which we live has its double and counterpart in the realm of spirits. A man lives here and his *chi* there. Indeed the human being is only one half (and the weaker half at that) of a person.' (Achebe, 1998, p.68)

Achebe further added, talking about the role of *chi* in human existence: 'No matter how many divinities sit together to plot a man's ruin it will come to nothing unless his chi is there among them.' Clearly chi has unprecedented veto powers over man's destiny (p.69).

Okpala added that 'The well-being of a person depends significantly on his relationship with his chi, on how his choice of action is influenced by his chi, on how much he displeases or appeases his chi' (2002, p.561).

A great characteristic of *chi* is that there is a good and a bad version of it, ezigbo and ajo. This is not a moral goodness, but a measure of how fortunate the one hosting it is going to be in life. In Igbo cosmology, whenever something good happens to somebody, people will say, "onya nwere ezigbo chi" – this person has a good *chi*. The reverse is also true; when something bad happens to someone, people will say, "onwere ajo chi" – he has a bad *chi*.

Achebe explained the phenomenon thus:

A man of impeccable character may yet have a bad chi so that nothing he puts his hand to will work out right. Chi is therefore more concerned with success or failure than with righteousness and wickedness. Which is not to say that it is totally indifferent to morality (Achebe, 1998, p.69).

In the novel, Chinonso's guardian spirit, defending himself, says 'Ebubedike, although I was greatly shaken by this, I was mightily relieved that my host was alive. If this man had killed him, what would his ancestors have said of me? Would they have said that I, his chi, was asleep? Or that I was an ajoo-chi? (Obioma, 2019,p.341).

This defence is not enough to exonerate *Chi* as not being an ajoo-chi. On the contrary, there is a lot in the novel that points out that it is in fact a bad *chi*. We can see this when we examine the previous lifecycles of Chinonso's *Chi*, especially if we focus on the love lives of those humans.

On page 60 of the novel, we see *Chi* recounting the sad end of one of his numerous human hosts:

> Egbunu! For I have seen many times that people, after their beloveds have left them, try to reclaim them as one would attempt to reclaim property that had been stolen. Wasn't this the case with Emejuiwe, who, one hundred and thirty years ago, killed the man who took his wife from him? (p. 60)

Recalling another incident from his previous existence, *Chi* said,

> ... whenever he sat by her, she'd say, 'Have I told you about your great ancestors Omenkara and Nkpotu?' [...] Omenkara had refused a white man's attempt to take his wife and was hanged in the village square by the district commissioner. (Chukwu, I bore witness to this cruel event…) (p.153).

With these revelations, we can appreciate then why, on the very first day Chinonso made love to Ndali, an akaliogili, a vagabond spirit, visited him when he was asleep. The scene unfolds thus:

> ... around midnight, something shot through the wall with uncanny speed. [...] Then it morphed into a most frightening agwu – with a roachlike head and portly human body. I lunged forward at once and ordered it to leave. *But it gazed at me with eyes filled with hate, then stared mostly at my host's unconscious body* [Italics added] (pp.63-64).

There are two major points of significance in this visit. The first is that the visit occurred on the night Chinonso first had carnal knowledge of Ndali, because that act marked them as lovers. In Igbo cosmology, the first day of every event is the most important day. According to an Igbo proverb, if one cannot tell where the rain began to fall on one, one cannot tell where it will stop.

The second point is reflected in the behaviour of the vagabond spirit. The narration notes how it gazes with eyes filled with hatred at Chinonso's *Chi*. This happens because the spirit is witness to knowledge *Chi* should also possess but is in constant denial of: the fact that it is a bad *chi*. The love life of whoever hosts *Chi* is doomed. Being privy to this knowledge, the vagabond spirit feels nothing but absolute hatred for it. Perhaps *Chi* has even inhabited the human body of the vagabond spirit, cursed its love life and turned it into what it became, a spirit cut off from reincarnation. So, when it looks at the unconscious body of Chinonso, it essentially stares at and pities him, knowing what his end is going to be like. The vagabond spirit knows that Chinonso is but an akaliogili in the making. He is in fact only biding his time.

There are others forces which provide clues throughout Chinonso's life, forewarning him of how dangerous it would be for him to fall in love, given it would be a love fated to doom. For instance, on the first day Chinonso visits Ndali's parents, he forgets the gift he has bought for her father. In Igbo tradition, it is a gross and culpable neglect to visit one's potential in-laws without a gift. It is considered an insult and the beginning of a damaging relationship. Chinonso's Chi knows this, and recounts it thus:

> Egbunu, I must say here that this was one of the occasions in which I had wanted to remind him that he was forgetting the gifts. But I didn't because of your counsel: *let man be man*.... But this omission [...] strikes me with pangs of regret (Obioma, 2019, pp.110-111).

However, like any lover, Chinonso ignores seeing this as a way of nature imploring him to flee the relationship. Instead of discouraging him, it does the exact opposite. In fact, all the hurdles he experiences only strengthen the bond between the lovers. The ordeal becomes something great that is conquered in the name of love. Even when Chinonso is tortured, insulted and humiliated by Ndali's family, it becomes a reason for Chinonso to strive harder, to sacrifice more in order to be with the one he loves. Ndali notes this fact in a letter to Chinonso, telling him why he is the man of her dreams:

> … when I see the love you show to ordinary animals, I knew you will show me greater love, greater care, greater help, greater everything. This is why I love you Nonso [...] How many men in Nigeria or even all over the world can sell

everything they have for the sake of a woman? (p.321)

But all this love, no matter how it was nursed and nurtured, was bound to fail because Chinonso was host to a bad *chi*.

There is something else important to add here. Even though *chi* embodies determinism, in Igbo cosmology there is still freedom left to man. Achebe put it thus:

The Igbo believe that a man receives his gifts or talents, his character [...] before he comes into the world. It seems there is an element of choice available to him at that point; and that his chi presides over bargaining. Hence the saying 'Obu etu nya na chie si kwu', which we often hear when a man's misfortune is somehow beyond comprehension and so can only be attributable to an agreement he himself must have entered into, at the beginning, alone with his chi... (Achebe, 1998, p.69)

It is what led to this adage among the Igbos: "Onye kwe chi ya ekwe" – when one affirms, his *chi* will affirm too. In this, a *chi* acts as subordinate to the will of its host. In this light we can understand why, even though Chinonso's *Chi* is a bad *chi*, there is an instance of an extraordinary personality which *Chi* guided who didn't come to a nasty end. *Chi* recounts this about the man:

I guided an extraordinarily gifted man who read books and wrote stories, Ezike Nkeoye [...] And it was from him that I acquired much of what I now know (Obioma, 2019, p.58).

He is not the only man that *Chi* guided and transitioned successfully to alamnuo. We see this when *Chi* is defending itself to Chinonso's ancestors, claiming that Chinonso's ordeal isn't its fault. *Chi* points to the fact that it has guided many of Chinonso's ancestors who have successfully returned to the domain of their predecessors.

There is weight to its argument. There is, in Chinonso's nature, a seed which leads him to his own destruction. It is this fault that the others who have been guided by *Chi* don't have, which allows them to return successfully to the domain of their ancestors. Chinonso is a violent man. In the story, we see this mostly in two instances, prior to his attack on Ndali's property. Firstly, when Chinonso angrily kills his pet gosling, because someone stronger than him steals the bird. Secondly, he kills one of the hawks that is preying on his poultry:

> ... As he tied the bird to the tree, he spoke to it and all its kind – all who stole what people like him reared with their sweat, time and money. [...] Then he struck the nail into its throat with the stone until the nail burst out on the other end (Obioma, 2019, p.94).

For a man capable of this, it perhaps isn't surprising that he would resort to violence as a means of punishing Ndali for leaving him and marrying another man. Chinonso ends up destroying himself not just because of his destiny but through the actions of his own free will. Chinonso's love was fated to tragedy and his free actions brought this fate about.

Mixing up free will and determinism as per Igbo Metaphysics is not a contradiction; it is a plausible paradox. We can conclude this part of the essay by explaining this conundrum through the words of Martin Buber:

> Destiny and freedom are solemnly promised to one another.

Only the man who makes freedom real to himself meets destiny ... destiny confronts him as the counterpart of his freedom. It is not his boundary, but his fulfilment; freedom and destiny are linked together in meaning (Buber, 1970, p.53)

Tragic lovers in *The Concubine*: Fated or Chosen?

Staying with Igbo Metaphysics, *The Concubine* (1966) takes a different view on whether tragic lovers choose, or are fated, to be together. *The Concubine* is fatalistic in its discussion of what happens when one is bonded in love:

'There are few women like that in the world', Anyika continued. 'It is death to marry them….'
'Is there nothing we can do to make the marriage work?'
'Nothing.'(Amadi, 1966, p.196)

Ignoring this advice, the young lover Ekwueme tries his best to evade fate. That is what happens with love – it removes normal logic. What Ekwueme does next, is to seek advice from another native doctor, one that will suit his desire to unite him in marriage with the woman he loves. When the second native doctor promises him the possibility of changing his fate, Ekwueme grabs the opportunity with both hands.

The novel captures the arrival of the native doctor as such:

Agwoturumbe the dibia arrived with a great flourish [...] He walked with a swagger [...] As he passed through Omakachi old men sitting in their reception halls hailed him (p. 206).

This glamourous entry would soon become mournful, as the ritual he conducts to save Ekwueme and his lover isn't enough, or will never be enough, to divert the hands of fate. Ekwueme would be accidentally killed by an arrow meant for a lizard. Ekwueme, like the rest of the lovers who had courted Ihuoma, would meet with a sudden death – a fate reserved for them all.

In *An Orchestra of Minorities*, we argued that the main character, Chinonso, meets his tragic end not just because he is destined to it, but because he himself, by choice, lived a life that merited such a fate.

In *The Concubine*, the reverse can be said of Ekwueme. Ekwueme is the ideal man, loved by everyone, the sort of laidback man which Nigerians refer to as 'husband material'. He is so well behaved that mothers long for him to be the husband of their daughters. A scene in the novel captured him thus:

> 'You will ruin your health fretting over your dead husband. I am worried about you, my daughter.'
> 'I cannot forget him so soon. He died only a year ago. I shall remain in his house and look after his children until they are grown. Then perhaps I may think of other things.'
> Okachi tried to persuade her daughter.
> 'Ekwueme is a well-behaved young man. I think I mentioned him when we were cooking.' (Amadi, 1966, p.40)

There are good reasons why mothers would wish for Ekwueme to be the husband of their daughters. Ekwueme has a big heart; he is that go-to person the villagers approach when in need. When Nnadi needs help to repair the roof of his dead brother's wife's house, he goes to Ekwueme and his friend Wodu Wakiri.

> 'I shall work on Ihuoma's roofs tomorrow,' Nnadi announced

to his wife as he made thatches in his reception hall.
[...]
'I shall invite Ekwueme and his friend Wodu Wakiri the wag
to help. I am sure Ekwueme would certainly come.' (Amadi,
1966, p.42)

As well as a man of goodwill, Ekwueme is popular in his
village. He is a good dancer, performing in every festival to
the admiration of all. He also has an enviable reputation as the
best hunter. Although he is not so good at wrestling, he is not
a weakling and has won some wrestling matches. One of the
greatest virtues he has is that he understands duty and is willing
to sacrifice his personal interests for the obligations imposed
on him by tradition. This is an admirable quality in the context
of the conservative environment he grew up in. Even though
Ekwueme had indicated his love for Ihouma, when duty called,
and his parents insisted that he had to marry the woman he had
been promised to since childhood, at first he fought, but later
gave in to maintain the tradition.

Unfortunately, none of these qualities will save him from
fate and his tragic end, once bonded with Ihuoma, because
Ekwueme's *Chi* is a bad *chi*. No matter how good Ekwueme
is, his ajoo chi means that he will never end up with anything
but sadness. An Igbo adage captured it thus: "Onyechi ya keri
agu naku agu" – he who is destined by his *chi* to bush must go
to the bush.

Conclusion

The fatalism in both novels comes from the nature of the chi
but, in *An Orchestra of Minorities* (2019) Obioma argues
through his narrative that there is active participation in the

form of both the chi and human agency feeding into what the individual's fate will be. In *The Concubine* (1966), it was a passive, absolute submission to the will of destiny. The only freedom afforded to the human actor is the choice of whether to fall in love or not. Because, once one falls in love with the heroine of the story, they have set up a necessarily determinist end that will most certainly come to pass. To be in love in *The Concubine* is to be bonded to fate and an unalterable tragic end, no matter how much character the individual displays.

There is a major problem with this though, as it removes moral responsibility. In light of this, if one errs in a relationship, say by cheating or killing a partner, the offender is beyond good and evil, since it has already been predetermined that they would do so.

On these grounds, we could say that, even though the two novels base the logic of their narratives on Igbo Metaphysics, Obioma gives a more plausible and open answer to the question of what happens to tragic lovers when they are bonded in love, and whether it was fated or chosen by them.

It is important to note here too that a charge can be made against the concept of 'chi' as used in explaining the notion of freedom and determinism in the novels. This charge comes in the shape of calling the idea of 'chi' a form of supernatural metaphysics. But if the whole argument of freedom and determinism in philosophy foregrounds the notion of God's omnipotence, then it is only the individual using different criteria to judge a similar concept who *will make* a distinction between God metaphysics and chi as supernatural metaphysics.

But the merit of the two different narratives being drawn from the same oral source, though argued in different directions, is that it serves as a criticism for those who think that traditional thought, or the philosophy of the village, is that of a herd mentality. We can learn from what Obioma and Amadi did, and conclude that oral literature is robust enough to sustain the interplay of divergent views in dialectical struggle, aiming to get closer to our understanding of reality.

Bibliography

Amadi. E., 1966. *The Concubine.* Oxford: Heinemann Publisher.

Bubel, M., 1970. *I and Thou.* Translated by Walter Kaufman. New York: Charles Scribner and Sons.

Chinua, A., 1998. Chi in Igbo Cosmology. In E.C. Eze, ed. 1998. *Africa Philosophy: An Anthology.* Oxford: Blackwell Publisher.

Edeh, E.M.P., 1985. *Towards an Igbo Metaphysics.* Chicago: Loyola University Press.

Okpala, J.C., 2002. Igbo Metaphysics in Chinua Achebe's "Things Fall Apart". *Callaloo*, Vol. 25, No. 2 (Spring, 2002), pp.559-566.

Obioma. C., 2019. *An Orchestra of Minorities.* London: Little Brown Publisher.

Hegel, G.W.F., 1884. *Lectures on the Philosophy of History.* Translated by J. Sibree. London: George Bell and Sons.

Yancy, G., 2004. *What White Looks Like: African-American Philosophers on the Whiteness Question.* London: Routledge.

Outlaw, L.T, 2017. Africana Philosophy. Available at <https://plato.stanford. edu/entries/africana/> [Accessed 8 September 2019].

Gormenghast and the Groans

Barbara Stevenson

Abstract

Stories need a strong focal point, whether it is an idea, character or place that is able to connect the various threads. In the *Titus Groan*/*Gormenghast* novels by Mervyn Peake it is Gormenghast, the ancestral home of the Groan family. Gormenghast Castle is surrounded by a forest leading to Gormenghast Mountain, which serves to cut the inhabitants off from reality. The castle is not merely a building: it is the heart of the story. The characters may love it or hate it, but it demands their complete devotion and they cannot ignore it. Neither is it impartial, sometimes helping the inhabitants, sometimes destroying them. It binds the Groan family to its stone walls with ties that are stronger than those of blood. This article considers the impact the castle has on the development of the eponymous hero, Titus Groan, through the influence it exerts over him and his close family members.

Introduction

Mervyn Peake wrote three novels in the Gormenghast series: *Titus Groan* (1946); *Gormenghast* (1950) and *Titus Alone* (1959). He left notes for a fourth novel, *Titus Awakes* (Gilmore, 2011) which was completed after his death by his widow Maeve Gilmore. The books follow the life of Titus Groan from his birth and early years in the first novel, his schooling in the second, his journeys in the third and his final destination in the fourth. This article concentrates on the first two novels, both set within Gormenghast, where Titus' character was shaped.

Mervyn Peake is not unique in confining the action of a novel to one specific location, in this case a Gothic castle. Comparisons with Kafka's *The Castle* (Kafka, 1926) and Peacock's *Nightmare Abbey* (1818) come to mind. Both have a Gothic feel and in both the stories revolve around the settings, but the castle and the abbey remain as buildings. In Peake's novels, Gormenghast is a character in its own right. Throughout the novels there are references to the building have body parts; for example a back (1950, p.14), a heart (1950, p.17), and a jaw (1950, p.46). It has a soul (1950, p.14), it broods (1950, p.7) and it is able to elicit feelings of love, as in the case of the villain Steerpike declaring:

"This is a *place*…without any doubt, this is *somewhere*." (1950, p.258. My emphasis).

It can also instil hatred. Fuchsia says she hates the world. (Peake, 1946, p.146). As she has never left the castle grounds, her world is Gormenghast.

The ruling family of Gormenghast is the Groan family and has been for centuries, presumably from the origin of the castle. The librarian, Barquentine, reflects that "…his veneration for the Earl (as a descendant of the original line) disassociating itself from his feelings about the man himself." (1946, p.448).

The family and their retainers are bound together by the castle and by a series of ridiculous rituals tied up in its history. Positions and duties are dictated by arcane rules.

> The walls of the vast room… were the personal concerns of a
> company of eighteen men known as the 'Grey Scrubbers'. It
> had been their privilege on reaching adolescence to discover
> that, being the sons of their fathers, their careers had been
> arranged for them and that stretching ahead of them lay their

identical lives consisting of an unimaginative if praiseworthy duty. (Peake, 1946, p.27)

Relationships depend upon the castle's hierarchical system; therefore Fuchsia, Lord Groan's daughter, and Steerpike, a castle servant, are forced to keep their romantic affair a secret.

"That she, the daughter of the Line, should see so much of an officer of the castle, for unofficial reasons, was, she knew, a crime against her station." (Peake, 1950, p.344)

It could be argued that the Groans do not own Gormenghast, but that Gormenghast owns the Groans.

Titus Groan, the 77th Earl in waiting, is the protagonist of the novels, although in the first novel his role is limited owing to his young age. In the second book his development is formed by the castle and by his family, who themselves have been influenced by Gormenghast. To understand Titus and his love/hate relationship to his ancestral home, which results in his escape, it is necessary to untangle the emotional web linking the entire family, beginning with his father, Lord Sepulchrave Groan.

Lord Sepulchrave Groan

Sepulchrave Groan is the 76th Earl of Gormenghast. Despite being the head of the family and lord of the castle he is a passive character, a slave to duty, bullied by the Master of Rituals. The castle has him in its grasp.

How could he love this place? He was part of it. He could not imagine a world outside it, and the idea of loving Gormenghast would have shocked him. To have asked him of his feelings for his hereditary home would be like asking a man what his feelings were towards his own hand or throat. (Peake, 1946, p.62)

He suffers from severe depression and is rarely mentioned without the epithet 'melancholic'. In some ways he bears a resemblance to Roderick Usher in Edgar Allan Poe's *The Fall of the House of Usher* (Poe, 1839). Like Sepulchrave, Usher is descended from a single line (p.92) and he suffers from a mental disorder connected to the family (p.93). Both men become obsessed with dying in their ancestral homes.

Adding to Sepulchrave's depression, before the story begins, is the fear he has harboured at his failure to produce a male heir and, having no brothers, consequently he would be responsible for the dying out of the line. (Peake, 1946, p.296). He does have a fifteen-year-old daughter, Fuchsia, but genealogically women are unimportant and he has little contact with her. On one occasion, meeting her at a castle ritual, he asks where she has been for the last fortnight. (p.51).

His marriage to Gertrude is a passionless one. He feels intellectually superior to her, but is cowed by her vitality and jealous of the attention she gives to her cats and wild birds. Their union is one of convenience, with the main aim being to produce an heir. (p.205)

When Titus is finally born it is a great relief to Sepulchrave, as it is to the castle as a whole. His depression begins to lift and he shows signs of interest and paternal pride. He interrupts Sourdust, the Master of Rituals, to ask "…have you heard about my son?" knowing that Sourdust knew everything that went on in the castle, but hoping for an encouraging response to the fact that he had fulfilled his duty as progenitor. (p.67). He makes an effort to see his son and collects fir cones for him to play with (p.227), but he finds he is unable to love the child as a person, only as a symbol of the continuation of the family name and the castle traditions. It vital that there is instilled in the boy a love for his birthplace and heritage and he instructs the nanny to make it a priority. (Peake, 1946, p.228).

At the same time as his burden has apparently lifted, Sepulchrave becomes aware that with the birth of an heir, his own tenure as Earl of Gormenghast is coming to a close.

The image of the circle or wheel of life is echoed in many novels and put succinctly in Russell Hoban's surreal fantasy The Lion of Boaz-Jachin and Jachin-Boaz. (Hoban, 1973, p.132) "…it must die because it has had children and is no longer needed."

Gormenghast itself decides that Sepulchrave, despite being a loyal servant, is no longer of use. Sepulchrave's one true love is for his library, which he considers his realm. (Peake, 1946, p.203). This is burnt down in an arson attack by Sepulchrave's jealous sisters, the twins Clara and Cora, spurred on by the upwardly mobile kitchen boy Steerpike. The castle conspires to make the task simpler for them, allowing the flames to catch and spread. As Steerpike says: "Nothing could have gone more deliciously to plan." (pp.316-320).

With the library gone, Sepulchrave's depression descends into madness and he believes he is a death owl. He perches on the mantelpiece hooting and eating mice. (pp.365-367). This brings him closer to his daughter for a brief period as she tries to help him and they share moments of deep love for one another.

"…she was affected by an uprising of love… For the first time in her life she felt that she was a daughter-that she had a father-of her own." (p.346-7).

It is too little, too late and Sepulchrave sacrifices himself one night to be devoured by the owls in the Tower of Flints in his "hour of re-incarnation". (p.440)

His family are unaware of the manner of his death and his disappearance is a mystery. They have no sympathy with his plight, and he is forever branded a renegade and a traitor to Gormenghast. (Peake, 1946, p. 447-448)

Sepulchrave's death brings the first novel to a close. Titus has ascended to the title of 77th Earl of Groan at the age of two. His development in the second novel is bound up with his aunts' action and his father's death, but he has had no personal knowledge of events, learning about them from castle servants and from his sister Fuchsia, who is his closest friend.

Fuchsia Groan

Titus' elder sister Fuchsia is earmarked as the Peter Pan (Barrie, 1911) of Gormenghast. She is fifteen when Titus is born, (Peake, 1946, p.51) although later claims to have been fourteen, (Peake, 1950, p.314) and there is a constant confusion about her actual age. When Titus is 'nearly eight' (p.43), Fuchsia is apparently only twenty (p.145) and at her death Titus is seventeen (p.424), which should make Fuchsia thirty-one or thirty-two, but she acts in the same childish manner that she did when Titus was born. Although some of the confusion may be accidental on the author's part, it gives the impression that the castle itself is preventing Fuchsia from growing up, enjoying having her as a caged pet. Her nanny says "You never listen, nor grow any older" (Peake, 1946, p.198) and her friend Dr. Prunesquallor considers her slow of speech with an almost irritating simplicity. (p.181).

Fuchsia rarely sees her parents, who show no affection towards her, and she has no friends of her own age. She is constantly reminded that she is only a girl and girls don't matter. (p.486) Only boys go to school and Fuchsia, as well as having no companions, has a poor education, relying on her simple nanny and whatever books she has found. She is, however, aware of her situation. She tells her brother: "…I've read quite a lot and I know that most children see a good deal of their parents – more than we do, anyway." (Peake, 1950, p.314).

It is hardly surprising that she has invented a childish fantasy hideout in the attic above her rooms. It is a space only she inhabits and one that she loves. (Peake, 1946, p.77). It is pertinent that this private space is defiled by the youth Steerpike, because as the story advances, his intentions are to seduce and defile Fuchsia herself in order to gain control of Gormenghast.

"With the death of Titus and Fuchsia in his power, the Countess alone would stand between him and a virtual dictatorship" (Peake, 1950, p.349).

Fuchsia abandons her attic soon after finding Steerpike there. The place is no longer sacrosanct.

Her mother Gertrude has no time for Fuchsia, blaming her for being a girl and "of little consequence in the eyes of the castle." (p.452). The situation is not helped by Fuchsia's aunts, Clarice and Cora, constantly feeding her their hatred of her mother. After Fuchsia's death, Titus accuses his mother of never loving Fuchsia, a charge which she does not deny. Yet she touchingly rearranges the sheet covering her daughter's body, fearing her child might feel the cold, (p.462) and personally finds the best place for her burial.

Fuchsia's relationship with her father blossoms as his mental health declines, possibly because his behaviour is becoming more childlike, which she can relate to. She is aware he wanted her to be a boy, and with the birth of Titus this disappointment is lifted. After her father's disappearance, she receives a new understanding of her place in the family; however with this realisation comes a melancholia. It is as if the castle, seeing that Fuchsia's eyes are being opened, intends to keep her within its grasp.

At the birth of her brother, Fuchsia was initially outraged, fearing her world was being torn apart, but she soon grows to love and protect him as an elder sister would. Despite the age difference, they become good friends and confidantes. This changes when Steerpike becomes serious in his pursuit of her. At heart, Fuchsia is a romantic, not having any experience of responsibility or reality. This makes it easy for Steerpike, a young man only two years older than she is, to seduce her. Flattered by his attention, Fuchsia's emotions are clouded and she cannot see his evil intentions. She believes her love for him is reciprocated. Titus has hated and mistrusted Steerpike from a young age, but Fuchsia will not tolerate anything bad said about Steerpike. Her relationship with her brother cools and she distances herself from him.

When Steerpike's true nature is revealed she is devastated, but has no-one to turn to. She has no relationship with her mother. Steerpike has poisoned her loyal nanny and murdered her childhood friend Mr. Flay. The doctor, who in the past had acted in loco parentis and listened to her troubles, is busy with the injuries and illnesses caused by the severe flooding and Steerpike's reign of terror. She contemplates suicide, while sitting on her windowsill looking down at the rising flood water. She is at the point of changing her mind when there is a sudden knock on her door. Startled by this, she falls into the water and drowns.

This melodramatic end seems fitting for Fuchsia. Gormenghast will survive Steerpike's treachery, the floods and Titus' betrayal, but it will not be the same. The castle, like a loving parent, is sparing Fuchsia from the horrors of reality. Or perhaps, like a jealous guardian, it is fearful that she may wish to leave with her brother and intends to prevent this at all costs.

Fuchsia's position in the castle is reminiscent of the little yellow bird in the song *Goodbye Little Yellow Bird* (William, 1903) – a prisoner in a cage of gold.

Clarice and Cora Groan

Apart from as a baby, Titus never meets his aunts, Sepulchrave's twin sisters Clarice and Cora. As young women they simultaneously suffered strokes, paralysing them on one side of their bodies. Subsequently they combine to perform tasks. They are bound to Gormenghast by their lineage, but even if the opportunity to leave arose, it is doubtful they would have taken it. They seek recognition and crave power, but feel cheated. Being women, they are ignored in favour of their brother, yet it is not Sepulchrave they turn against, but his wife Gertrude.

"'Get on in life?' said Lady Cora at once, 'get on in life … What chance have we when Gertrude has what we ought to have.'" (Peake, 1946, p.110)

They feel she is an outsider who has usurped the place of honour they deserve. Although they attend some family rituals, they mainly keep to their own rooms, brooding in silence. At Titus' christening, Gertrude asks:

"'Where have you been since then?'" referring to Fuchsia's christening, fourteen or fifteen years previously. "'We've been in the south wing all the time, Gertrude,' replied Cora." (p.113)

Their desire for revenge on Gertrude, coupled with their inability to take action, makes it easy for Steerpike to manipulate them.

"Here, from the mouth of a stranger, their old scores and grievances were being aired and formulated." (Peake, 1946, p.255)

Acting as a loyal servant, Steerpike incites their hatred towards the rest of their family, flatters them and makes false promises, persuading them to burn Sepulchrave's library as a warning not to ignore them. He sets everything up; all the twins need do is light the wick. Once they have done this, and Steerpike emerges as the hero, saving the family who unbeknown to the twins are inside, he blackmails them into silence. Finally he convinces them that a deadly plague has taken over Gormenghast. They cut themselves off from the rest of the castle and move to a disused dungeon for safety, where Steerpike leaves them to rot. When the family eventually realise they haven't seen the twins for an overly long period of time, Steerpike forges a suicide note and the twins are believed to have drowned themselves.

Paradoxically, it is not Gormenghast that has abandoned or rejected the twins. They may be inconsequential, but they are of the Groan line. It is their stubbornness and inflated egos that isolate them. They could easily have found a role in castle life, supporting Fuchsia with her education, taking an interest in their brother's books or arranging much needed parties and social functions to lighten the air. Instead, like Miss Havisham in *Great Expectations* (Dickens, 1861), they feel Gormenghast has jilted them in favour of Gertrude and they separate themselves from castle life, failing to move on emotionally. The effect is the reverse of the desired one. The castle feels betrayed by the twins and allows them to suffer, almost taking a malign pleasure as they starve to death. Flay hears noises and searches for the source, at one point being a mere few feet away from finding and rescuing them, but the castle will have none of it. (Peake, 1950, p.301-2)

Countess Gertrude Groan

Titus' mother is an outsider who has married into the family. It is not stated where she came from, but since there are no other high-class families in Gormenghast, the reader assumes she came from outside the castle. There is no reference to anyone on her side of the family. Having arrived, the castle accepts her and she becomes an integral part of Gormenghast.

There is no love between her and her husband Sepulchrave, but she has a deep passion for Gormenghast and its traditions.

> Her husband was going mad. She had never loved him and she did not love him now, her heart being awakened to tenderness only by her birds and her white cats. But though she did not love him for himself, her unthinking and rooted respect for the heritage which he personified and her dumb pride in the line of his descent had filled her since her discovery of his illness. (Peake, 1946, p.413-414)

Like her husband, she had a fear of the Groan line ending through her.

"..it is good that Titus is born for the line of the Groans must never be broken through me and there must be no ending at all…" (p.399)

Although the point of the marriage was to produce children, Gertrude's maternal instincts are suppressed to a state almost of nonexistence. She makes no secret of the fact that she has no time for Fuchsia, because she is a girl.

"I have never taught Fuchsia because I have kept my knowledge for the boy." (p.398).

When Titus is born, she immediately hands him over to Nanny Slagg, who she instructs to find a wet nurse and tells her to "bring him back when he is six." (Peake, 1946, p.61). In the introduction to the second book, *Gormenghast*, it is stated that she saw her son seven times in seven years. (Peake, 1950, p.12) As he grows from a boy into a young man, she finds it difficult to relate to him.

"'Yes mother,' said Titus. The word mother had perplexed her. But the boy was quite right, of course." (p.315).

Later, when Titus overcomes the traitor Steerpike and restores order to Gormenghast, she is proud of his achievement, but is unable to tell him this.

"His mother had nothing to say to him. She had become even more withdrawn. Her pride in the courage he had shown had emptied her of words." (p.505).

It would be a misnomer to say that Gertrude was without love. She has a fierce passion for wild birds and her white cats. She reads fairy tales aloud to her cats with what is expressed as childlike wonder. (Peake, 1946, p.297)

After her husband's death it is Gertrude who takes over as the castle's protector.

"There is perfidy... I will break it: not only for Titus' sake and for his dead father's, but more – for Gormenghast." (Peake, 1950, p.43)

Indeed, her only act of treachery to the castle and its traditions was to dismiss her husband's loyal manservant Flay, because in a pique of rage he had thrown one of her cats at the evil Steerpike. She had regrets, but her cats came first.

"...and though she would no more have thought of recalling him than of ceasing to tend the cat which he had bruised, yet she was aware of having uprooted a part of Gormenghast." (Peake, 1946, p.414)

Such is her faith in Gormenghast, she cannot believe that her son would wish to leave and considers him weak and a traitor, like his father.

"'Going where?' she said at last. 'There's not a road, not a track, but it will lead you home. For everything comes to Gormenghast.'" (Peake, 1950, p.510)

Her faith in the castle is rewarded, as she is the one who remains and is entrusted with carrying on the Gormenghast traditions.

Titus Groan

Despite being the eponymous hero of the first novel, Titus is a mere baby and his role is a passive one. The book is about Gormenghast and serves to set the scene for Titus' development and subsequent actions. The second novels charters Titus' life from age two until he reaches manhood and leaves Gormenghast and it could be argued that the titles of the books should be reversed. Yet being the heir, even as a baby, he is the life of the castle. Everything revolves around him. From the moment he is born, the continuation of the Groan line is transferred onto his shoulders.

At the same time, his birth marks the escape from the kitchen of Steerpike and the beginning of his plan to take control of the castle. Titus likes being considered special and feted by everyone around him. He rejoices in finding a part of the castle that has been unexplored for centuries. "This is mine! mine!' he said aloud." (Peake, 1950, p.50) However, he is not willing to shoulder the responsibilities that go with the position, and in response the castle puts forward Steerpike as a rival to test him.

There is little love in Titus' young life. His father is dead and his mother is cold. Nanny Slagg, who adored him as a baby, is poisoned by Steerpike. He shares a bond with his sister Fuchsia, despite her being fifteen years older than he is, and is devastated by her death. He also has a foster sister, the daughter of his wet nurse, who he lusts after, but she is killed by lightning.

Because of this lack of warmth in his formative years, he comes across as a selfish, uncaring boy. In later years he finds it difficult to feel love for others, abandoning a pregnant lover in *Titus Awakes* (Gilmore, 2011, pp.36-37).

Titus feels trapped by Gormenghast and he hates the castle and all it stands for. Mistaken in the belief that Steerpike murdered his sister Fuchsia, his actions in defence of Gormenghast are his way of seeking revenge. They have nothing to do with loyalty to the castle. Once Steerpike is dead and the flood consuming the castle has abated, Titus abandons his home and his mother. At the end of *Titus Alone*, the third book in the series, he finds himself on the far side of Gormenghast Mountain. He can feel home and knows, should he skirt the base of the rock, he would be able to see it, but chooses not to return there.

"He had no longer any need for home, for he carried his Gormenghast within him." (Peake, 1959, pp.262-3)

His relationship to Gormenghast is similar to that portrayed in the song *Wand'rin' Star* (Lerner, 1951) in the Broadway production of *Paint Your Wagons* (Lerner, 1951) and later the movie. (*Paint Your Wagons*, 1969)

"Home is made for coming from, for dreams of going to, which with any luck will never come true." (Lerner, 1951, song *Wan'rin' Star*, lines 8 and 9)

Conclusion

To an outsider the Groans are a cold, dysfunctional family. They rarely interact with one another and it seems surprising that such a family could have survived for generations. The one, powerful thing that binds them together is Gormenghast. Each in their way has a bond of devotion to the castle. Sepulchrave loves Gormenghast as a soldier loves his country and flag. He sacrificed any dreams and ambitions he might have had to adhere to pointless duties, whose meaning had been lost centuries before. Clarice and Cora see Gormenghast as a prized possession to be cherished. They burn themselves out with dreams of being the castle's master. Fuchsia is denied a proper childhood, yet she willingly assumes the role of an eternal child, refusing to grow up. She is in love with a fairy tale. Gertrude, although an outsider, takes up the role of battle-scarred general when called upon by the castle. A stone lion atop part of the castle's east wing holds the corpse of a man in its jaws with the words 'He was an enemy of Groan' chiselled on the man's body (Peake, 1946, p.202). She takes this motto to heart, losing her daughter in the process and having her son betray her.

Even Titus, who professes to hate Gormenghast and escapes from the castle, opens his heart to Ruth, one of his lovers, by talking to her about "– the castle – all that it stood for – all that at times he could hardly breathe for the longing for..." (Gilmore, 2011, p.163)

It is somehow fitting that Maeve Gilmore chose to end Titus Awakes with an adaptation of the words Gertrude uses at the end of Gormenghast.

"There's not a road, not a track, but it will lead him home." (Gilmore, 2011, p.265)

Bibliography

Barrie, J. M., 1911. *Peter and Wendy*. London: Hodder and Stoughton.

Dickens, C., 1861. *Great Expectations*. London: Chapman and Hall.

Gilmore, M., 2011. *Titus Awakes*. New York: Random House.

Hoban, R., 1973. *The Lion of Boaz-Jachin and Jachin-Boaz*. Picador, London 1974 ed. s.l.:s.n.

Kafka, F., 1926. *The Castle*. Minerva 1992 ed. London: s.n.

Lerner, A. J. F. L., 1951. *Wand'rin' Star*. [Sound Recording].

Peacock, T. L., 1818. *Nightmare Abbey*. Penguin Classics, London 1986 ed. s.l.:s.n.

Peake, M., 1946. *Titus Groan*. Penguin Books 1980 ed. s.l.:Eyre and Spottiswoode.

Peake, M., 1950. *Gormenghast*. Penguin Books 1980 ed. s.l.:Eyre and Spottiswoode.

Peake, M., 1959. *Titus Alone*. Penguin Books 1980 ed. s.l.:Eyre and Spottiswoode.

Poe, E. A., 1839. The Fall of the House of Usher. *The Fall of the House of Usher and Other Writings*, Penguin Classic 2003 ed. s.l.:s.n.

William, C., 1903 music by W H Murphy. *Goodbye Little Yellow Bird* [Sound Recording].

Clothing as a Reflection of Love in the Chivalric Novels of the 14th and 15th Centuries in Catalonia

Dr. Ester Torredelforth

Abstract

Fashion has always been established as a semiotic tool in which both the personality and the emotional state of the person are expressed. Nowadays, and practically since the origins of humanity, it has been possible to show, through dressing, the state of loving and belonging to another human being. Chivalric novels of the fifteenth century provide a wide sample of how, in medieval society, lovers used their clothes and garments to give signs and encoded messages of their love, show the inclinations of their hearts, or the possession of the affection of another person, be it in secret or public. These aspects will be analysed through the central novels of the fourteenth and fifteenth centuries, as well as contrasted with our knowledge of colour symbologies in medieval clothing, gifted garments, the seduction games and the limits imposed by the morality of the moment. All this can show us that, deep down, things may not have changed that much in society since then.

*

"He wore that shirt and everyone knew he loved her."

Such a statement may sound strange, even daring, today, but six centuries ago it responded to a reality that itself had manifested. Can a single piece of clothing give such a direct and clear message? The history of clothing is an inexhaustible source of social semiotics, personal semiology, class idiosyncrasy and information on the economic situation of the moment that creates it. The garments and the materials with which they were made, as well as the styles chosen for their decoration, are now established as an access tool to understand the way of thinking of the people who wear them. Since historians have demonstrated to date the truthfulness of these statements in a broad way (Squicciarino, 1990, p.17), in the context of a publication like this one you could raise a question: can these types of codes be applied to Fantasy literature? Or even, would it be possible through its analysis for us to perceive in greater detail aspects of the story that would otherwise go unnoticed?

At present, and almost since the origins of humanity, it has been possible to show through dress the state of romantic belonging to another human being. The chivalric novels of the fourteenth and fifteenth century seem to give a broad sample of how in medieval society lovers used their clothes and garments to give away signs and keys of their love, show the inclinations of their hearts, or the possession of the affection of another person, whether secretly or publicly.

Chivalric novels throughout Europe are an invaluable source of fantastic literature from the very midst of the Middle Ages. In Catalonia, they were direct heirs of Arthuric literature, the *Materia bretanya* as it was called back then[1], as well as the

---

1. In the late Middle Ages there were three literary cycles or subjects that were considered essential reading: *Materia de Roma*, which included mythological themes of classical antiquity; *Materia de Francia*, which brought together the stories of the paladins of Charlemagne as well as their wars against Arabs and Saracens. And finally the *Materia de Bretaña*, whose main theme was the adventures of King Arthur as well as other lesser-known legendary stories all contextualized in the British Isles, such as those of *King Lear* and *Gogmagog*, *Bruto of Troy* or *Old King Coel*. Jean Bodel, an important French poet of the twelfth century, described in his work *Chanson des Saisnes* the importance of this by saying: "Ne sont que III matières à nul homme atandant, De France

troubadour creations of the moment. They arrived, usually, in Occitan language to the southern courts and delighted lovers and dreamers with stories and characters generally coming from the British lands and of incredible adventures.

The production of medieval literature belonging to the Catalan-Aragonese crown has its own evolution in that regard. This ranged from the totally fanciful chivalrous novels elaborated in verse – typical of the fourteenth century – to the long novels of chivalry that would arrive along the XV century. The latter had a more realistic style, close to Italian humanism in vogue at the time – though they didn't omit passages and allegorical details, and even featured stellar appearances from Arthurian characters (Martorell, 1490, vol I, p.415). In all of them, there can be found clear references to the fashion of the moment: *garlandas*, *gonellas*, typologies of specific dresses, materials and even shapes are mentioned. (Badia, 2003, pp. 94, 117). Thus, in this study, an exhaustive analysis will be elaborated regarding the love messages concealed in these types of clothing descriptions[2].

There seems to be four basic ways in which romance was shown in these types of novels: firstly, the gift of clothes and the showing of them; secondly, the elaboration and gift of jewellery; thirdly, the parity of lovers when it comes to dressing; and, finally, the use of colour as a symbol of romance or even of predisposition to it.

The implicit message in the aforementioned items cannot go unnoticed. An important example can be found in one of

et de Bretaigne, et de Rome la grant." ("There are three literary cycles that no man should lack: the matter of France, of Brittany, and of the great Rome.")
2. Regarding the mentions of clothing, there will be taken for granted a structure currently accepted within these studies in which clothing is understood as both garments and those ornaments that are typical of the production of accessories such as shoes and jewellery.

the main novels of the century, *Fraire-de-Joi e Sor-de-Plaser*, which tells the story of a princess, the daughter of the Emperor Gint-Senay, who is magically mired in sleep. To protect the latent body of their daughter, the emperors build around her a glass tower surrounded by an impregnable moat, in turn surrounded by a paradisiacal environment. The plot – which clearly prefigures the classic story of the sleeping beauty according to experts – tells that Fraire-de-Joi, the bold son of the king of Florianda, hears about the beauty and being of the princess, thus falling in love without even seeing her. With Virgil's help, he manages to enter the tower and reach her.

When the knight manages to reach the princess' room, he lifts the golden mantle that covers her and sees the princess in what would be understood as an undershirt[3] or nightshirt of the time. This detail that could easily be overlooked could be a strong clarification in a novel of the time: no one would ever show themselves to others in such a manner, neither maidens, nor young people, nor gentlemen. This was due to the fact that, although this fine garment covered the body, it was considered that the person was literally naked, to the extent that medieval nobility could not be seen publicly dressing in such a way, not even among the servants. Even in the novels of the moment there can be found expressions that clarify it in such way:

> ...al catiu ho donaren, lo qual, despullat, en camisa fonc mès en lo corral.

---

3. In this direction, it is not possible to move forward without recommending the extensive bibliography regarding the use of the shirt by women in the peninsular kingdoms during the fourteenth to fifteenth centuries. Carmen Bernis has a large and detailed article entitled *Indumentaria española del siglo XV: la camisa de mujer*, where she makes an analysis of the main details in this regard, completed by his great work *" al catiu ho donaren, lo qual, despullat, en camisa fonc mès en lo corral." (Anon., 1435-1462, p.297)* , in two volumes, which completes and delights those interested in the subject.

(… and they gave him to the captive, who, naked in his shirt, was put in the room.) (Anon., 1435-1462, p.297)

It was the first layer of clothing, the one that was in direct contact with the skin, the most intimate. We can thus understand a glimpse of this sensual and intimate moment that is orchestrated in the novel when Fraire-de-joi sees Sor-de-plaser 'in a shirt'.[4] The story thus suggests it when later, and ignited with passion with such a vision, the knight lies with the sleeping body of the princess, leaving her pregnant.

This garment was actually the favourite of the gentlemen because the ladies gave it as an intimate gift to their hidden lover, and, indeed, this custom is portrayed in the chivalric novels of the period.

*

The gift of clothes and the sample of them, is the first of the characteristics that stand out throughout the fantasy stories portrayed in the chivalric novels and the gift of the female shirt stands out in this direction. As an example, Güelfa gives Curial her shirt before the knight goes to war. In the novel that bears their names, written in the mid-fifteenth century, the love story is develop between the young widow of high lineage and Cürial, a knight of humble origins. This central work of Catalan chivalric literature portrays the classic troubadour

---

4. In medieval fashion, three groups of garments were established depending on their placement on the body: underwear, which were placed directly on the body; *de a cuerpo* or first layer garments, which were placed as the first layer, which were understood as the most basic; *de encima* or second layer garments, as a second layer that gave greater formality and was commonly worn indoors; and, finally, *de abrigo* or top layer garments as the last layer, generally designed for outdoor use.

romance in which a superior lady grants her love to a lesser knight. In this case, Güelfa will establish herself not only as the beloved but also as the benefactor, giving away even armour to Curial (Anon., 1435-1462, p.36). Among all the gifts she makes, her shirt stands out. The piece, also called *alcandora* (Marangues, 1991, pp.42,43), is described elaborated in *impla*, one of the finest and most precious fabrics of the moment to make this woman's garment (Martinez, 1989, pp.477-489). The loving gesture of this garment seems to be established in two directions in this case: the gift of this specific garment as well as the decoration that the lady elaborates on it. Nothing more intimate could be given to someone than a shirt, and knights and those around them were completely aware of it. Therefore, it was usually worn on top of the armour, as a clear and direct sign that the owner's heart was in somebody's possession.

In Joanot Martorell's work *Tirant lo Blanch*, written between 1450 and 1490, there is also a similar episode. The novel tells the adventures and rise of a knight named Tirant, who travels throughout Europe from England to Constantinople. There he will meet Carmesina, the emperor's daughter, with whom he will live an intense romance with a tragic ending, all combined with the love stories of other characters, deeds in battles and chivalrous adventures, which fill an extraordinarily extensive novel compared to those elaborated up to date. In it, the knight asks Carmesina for her shirt in order to wear it to battle, placing it on top of his armour (Martorell, 1490, vol I, pp.254-256). In the novel, an extremely revealing statement is made regarding this type of custom:

Sobre les tues armes he vist portar hàbit de doncella; postres, segons lo senyal, ésser enamorat d'ella
(On your weapons I see you have a maiden garment, you

show, then, a clear sign of being in love with her) (Martorell, 1490, vol I, p.313)

When we grasp the clear message that the gentleman was giving with this gesture, it sounds logical that, sometimes, knights – in reality and also in fiction – kept in secret the name of the garment's owner. Bernat Metge criticized this kind of custom in his book of moralistic literature *Lo Somni*:

> E açò que no els és menor vergonya, van ab alcandores brodades e perfumades, així com si eren donzelles qui deguessen anar a marit; e fan-les sobrepujar a les altres vestedures...
> (And in this that is no less embarrassing, they go with embroidered and scented alcandoras, as if they were maids who were going to get married; and make them overshoot over the other clothes...) (Badia and Lamuela, 1975, p.242)

Furthering the topic of Güelfa's shirt, and as a second detail, she and the abbess cover it with embroidered Sant Jordi's crosses, a possible reference to the desire for protection that the beloved wished upon the knight. The figure of Sant Jordi was central to the nobility of the moment and was established as further evidence of the extension of the chivalrous ideals in the ruling class of the moment, which reached beyond fantastic stories. Saint George was the saintly knight *par excellence*, and the nobility acquired him as his own representative and bulwark in the image of his own soul and will to be. The dragon's slayer would be established in Catalonia as patron of government institutions and as a holy protector of the nobility of Cavalry, even being embodied in the works of art of the moment (Macias and Cornudella, 2011-2012, p.24). It is understandable that Güelfa embroiders his crosses on his shirt, with the belief that

Curial will be protected in the battle that awaits him (Anon., 1435-1462, p.86).

The gift of intimate garments from ladies is sought by writers as a prime excuse to recreate funny situations based on confusion or wrong messages. One such instance is when the king of Tirant lo Blanch's novel finds a *camalliga*[5] of the maiden Madreselva on the ground and gladly places it on his leg oblivious to the fact he is implying, in front the entire court, that she is his beloved in secret. (Martorell, 1490, Vol I, p.147)

*

Beyond this, the gift and elaboration of jewels also appears as one of the most common and valued gestures among lovers of chivalrous novels of the moment. The gift of jewels as a present to the esteemed, loved ones or even people who have provided a useful service to a superior seems to have been an extended custom throughout the Middle Ages. In the context of courteous love, the lady was established as a superior and idealized being, before whom the knight submitted himself to the bonds of love. It was the lady, then, like a feudal lord, who most frequently gave the gifts to such a knight[6]. Many of these

---

5. The term designated a cord or ribbon used so that the shims or socks did not slip down the leg. This type of garment was mostly worn by males; that is why the king does not mind placing it on his own leg when it is a woman's garment according to the story. Women are also mentioned in the documentation but, since this garment was never seen, probably less importance was given to it according to the shortage of mentions. (Marangues, 1991, pp 47, 48).

6. In medieval times, the noble and feudal lords had the habit of giving gifts to knights and servitude. The kings gave valuable jewels to noblemen who had given a precious service to the crown. These types of gestures eventually became an unwritten rule, which was even present in the inheritance. Detailed portraits of the subject are made by authors such as Bonassie, Guichard or Gerbet in their work *Las Españas Medievales* (Bonassie, Guichard and Gerbet, 2001, p. 325)

valuable presents actually seemed to be delivered because of a separation, although the gift did not always respond to that occasion.

The novel *Blandín de Cornualla*, an anonymous story made between the thirteenth and fourteenth century in ancient Occitan, shows a good example of this and explains the deeds of a knight of British origins called Blandín. After different adventures, he arrives at a road where he finds a maiden who changes his horse for a white stallion. The animal leads him to a castle where Brianda sleeps under an enchantment. Her brother mentions that he must capture a white azore to wake her up. After defeating a dragon, an ogre and a giant snake, Blandín gets the bird, thus saving Brianda and later coming to his friend's aid, the knight Guillot Ardit de Miramar. Both end up marrying their respective ladies after having gained fame and experienced extraordinary events.

In the novel, maid Brianda gives Blandín a set of jewels called *joyeles*[7] before he goes on a final and dangerous adventure (Pacheco, 1983, pp.63, 67). Here we see a loving gesture, but her present is rejected by Blandín who, as an idealistic knight, shows that he does not wish for himself the riches of his beloved but only her company. This attitude is not equally imitated by his partner Guillot Ardit, who is established as a more earthly counterpoint character. (Pacheco, 1983, p.45)

Two seem to be the most common pieces of jewellery to

---

7. A term that was used to refer to a jewel of great value that was elaborated in different forms which could be hung on the neck or, after being detached, could also be placed as an ornament in hats, headbands or other places. (Yarza, 2003, p. 84). There were some pieces that where even named because of their great economic value. The *joyeles* were highly appreciated, and commonly used as gifts and as pawn parts in situations of need. There is an extensive account of the use of *joyeles* in the documentation. Some were valuable enough to relieve some kings of economic problems in harsh times during their reign. (Dalmases, 1992, vol. I, p. 36).

show these love relationships: rings and necklaces. We have good examples such as that of the Plaerdemavida maiden who, in *Tirant lo Blanch*, shows through a necklace to be married (Martorell, 1490, vol II, p.273). When he receives the first love letter from his beloved Güelfa, Sir Curial makes it sit in a necklace by putting the paper tightly rolled, wrapped in dark silk and embedded in a golden lion, which he always carries with him as a sign of love. (Anon., 1435-1462, p.53)

The rings have also been established since ancient times as one of the favourite gifts which imply a sign of affection and commitment. As a gift, they were extended to all social classes and it seems that, when not made in gold, they were produced in tin (Badia, 2003, p.124). Many of the medieval jewels carried engraved or carved messages, which were applied even on the clothing – rings were no exception either. In the novel *Fraire-de-Joi e Sor-de-Plaser*, the son of King Florianda exchanges his ring for the one of the sleeping maiden. The inscriptions of both are an internal message, and even a sample of the story to come. The ring of the maiden says: "'I am the ring of Sor-de-Plaser, / whoever has me may have her, / for love, with lively pleasure, / when she has fulfilled his joy'" and the ring of the knight prince says: "'I am the ring of Frayre de Joy, / the one who possesses me I will love, / not in the manner of a small man, / but as the son of a king'" (Badia , 2003, p.120). Both rings are used in the final meeting of the lovers: the princess recognizes the knight who woke her when she saw her own ring in her hand after the magical recovery (Badia, 2003, p.127)[8].

Tirant lo Blanch's novel mentions a ring which could

---

8. These types of inscriptions with messages were spread through the real fashion of the moment, being also worn on clothing even in languages such as Arabic or invented calligraphy that tried to imitate it. This is established as a topic still to be investigated, especially regarding Castilian and Catalan medieval fashion.

symbolize the concept of completion that the presence of the beloved brings to the person in love. Guillem de Varoïc's wife receives a gift from her husband: a double ring whose divided parts would be worn separately by each of them. Thus, the ring was established as a symbol of the completion of the lovers and the fulfillment of love only while they were together (Martorell, 1490, vol I, p.18). Is this not a way to mark the item as a jewellery set? In reality, this ring is only a small sample of all the clothes or objects carried by the lovers as a sign of loving possession.

*

Parity among lovers is a theme portrayed in the novels of chivalry, but it is not foreign to current generations. In the book on etiquette *Debrett's New Guide to Etiquette & Modern Manners*, a reference is made advising on how to behave properly for the new generations where the author reminds, as a clear recommendation, that couples should be easily associated with each other through dressing and image (Morgan, 2001, p.335). This idea, which in a book of manners does not go beyond a recommendation for elegance, was more than an option in medieval times.

In Catalan chivalry novels, it seems that this type of analogy was used – even beyond clothing many times – when matching the name of lovers, as in the case of Blandin and Brianda. Regarding jewellery pieces, the wide use of paired rings can be seen, either because of the message they carry, such as *Fraire-de-Joi e Sor-de-Plaser*, or because they are a single piece like the aforementioned ring of the Countess in *Tirant lo Blanch*.

However, what is the case with clothing? In Martorell's novel, for example, married couples are mentioned to be attending the royal parade – dressed in the same fabrics as their husbands – on the king's wedding with the princess of France. (Martorell, 1490, vol I, p.75.)

Perhaps one of the most representative passages is the one explained in *Curial e Güelfa*, where the character of Laquesis, a young noble maiden in love with Curial and rivalling Güelfa, is described as a jealous lady prone to intrigues, that promotes arguments between lovers subtly and using Curial's naivety. How? By giving the knight garments and fabrics made with her own fabric. Laquesis clothing is described as a white damask lined with ermine skin with an embroidered motif characteristic of her:

> Vestia aquest jorn Laquesis una roba de domàs blanc forrada d'erminis, tota brodada d'ulls, dels quals eixien llaços d'or fets en diverses maneres. E jatsia los llaços fossen buits, certes molts hi eren caiguts…
>
> (Laquesis wore a white damask clothing lined with ermine, all embroidered with eyes, from which gold ties came out made in different ways. And although the ties were empty, many were fallen ...) (Anon., 1435-1462, p.57)

With this fabric, Laquesis not only makes her dresses but also her tents, bedspreads and curtains, to such an extent that she is widely related by everyone to that design of ties and eyes. The strategy of Laquesis begins when she sends Curial the white clothes embroidered with her motifs, which he then uses to fashion his garments that he displays in front of everyone (Anon., 1435-1462, p.61). She gives him her high-value jewels, and he accepts them which, apparently, seems a subtle glimpse of indecision regarding his feelings for Güelfa or his own ambition for wealth (Anon., 1435-1462, p.146). It is in details like these that we might see how the 15th-century Catalan chivalry novel differs from the previous century, since it does not directly idealize the figure of the protagonist knight and begins to portray more complex, human and realistic characters. Curial is the ideal knight and the faithful lover despite being hesitant and at the same time ambitious.

At a certain point in the novel, Laquesis takes a step forward to claim even more ground in her struggle for Curial's attention and, along with her change of attitude, the colour of her clothes does so accordingly: from pure white to carmine red, always without losing the embroidered ties and eyes that characterize the design. She gives Curial a tent made with these fabrics and then she walks with clothes made of the same material, caching the attention of the king that relates her directly to Curial, asking the lady her relation with the courageous knight. The court assumes that at least they are known to each other through the parity of designs that bind them. The story explains:

> Vestia Laquesis una roba … tals com eren en la tenda que havia donada a Curial. E, com fos reconeguda, tothom dix:
> - Aquella roba e aquesta tenda tot és una cosa.
> Per què lo rei féu venir a Laquesis e dix:
> - Laquesis, la vostra roba me fa creure que vós devets conèixer lo cavaller de qui aquesta tenda és…
> (Laquesis wore a fabric… such as those in the tent she had given to Curial. And, as she was recognized, everyone said:
> - These clothes and this tent are the same thing.
> Because of this, the king made her come and said to Laquesis:
> - Laquesis, your clothes make me believe that you must know the knight who owns that tent ...)
> (Anon., 1435-1462, p.171-172)

This is used by the enemies of Curial, who falsely accuse him before the king of France and his beloved, causing the momentarily loss of their favour.

These types of tendencies seem to end up being reflected even in the colour that the names or nicknames of the protagonists in love in these stories reflect. Tirant is defined in the novel as "the white", probably a reference to the positive connotations of goodness and purity of intentions that are reflected in him. His love, on the other hand, is called *Carmesina*, referring to the intense red or scarlet colour. The name Carmesina is a derivation of the term *carmine*, in turn from the Arabic karmasī, (D.I.E.C.) widely used in the world of cosmetics to designate intense red lips. During the Middle Ages, it was the name given to the intense red dye that was obtained from Kermes, a parasite typically found in the young branches of the Mediterranean trees called *garrigas*. It represented for a long time the most expensive dye to produce these shades, since it gave a solid and intense colour. It was an extraordinarily expensive tonality to produce, just like pure intense white, and, over time, it also came to designate the dyed fabric of that colour. It was used by both sexes indifferently and is often mentioned in relation to descriptions of clothing (Marangues, 1991, pp114-115). In *Curial e Güelfa*, it is mentioned as follows:

> Vestia Laquesis una roba de setí ras carmesí.
> (Laquesis wore crimson satin clothing)
> (Anon., 1435-1462, p.171)

One of the most valued stones in those times, the ruby – by nature with crimson reflections – was used under the belief that it had magical and supernatural powers, granting honour and wealth to those who possessed it. It is then rather inevitable to ask: is it not ultimately wealth and honour that Tirant lo Blanch earns by possessing the love of Carmesina, the emperor's daughter? Many are the allegorical aspects and the hidden symbology in the use of names and their parity in the characters of the chivalry novels of this historical moment.

These details and symbolic relationships to materials and fabrics, which could go unnoticed nowadays by the contemporary reader, were easily and quickly identified by the consumers of medieval literature, who were accustomed to their constant use. For them, the message, although subtle, was direct.

*

The use of colour as a symbol of romance is the last characteristic that remains to be analysed. The colour symbology has been extensively studied to date, by authors who have focused both on their evolution in general and on their use during the medieval period[9]. Alison Laurie claimed, and rightly so, that the colour is to dressing what the tone is to the voice of the speaker. (Lurie, 1994, p.202) In chivalry novels, the allegorical use of both the characters and the descriptions was generalised. This symbology applied to clothing stands out and is one of the greatest sources of covert messages that could go unnoticed. Apparently, these messages were naturally deciphered by the contemporary medieval reader and even helped him to discern the direction that the adventures of the hero would take.

According to Pastoreau, before the fifteenth century, colour symbology was strongly developed around a triad of defined

9. In this regard, the research of Michelle Pastoreau must be mentioned, whose corpus of publications regarding the history of colour stands out today with books such as *Azul: historia de un color*, or *Las vestiduras del diablo: Breve historia de las rayas en la indumentaria* among others.

colours: white, red and black. White was used to symbolize purity, red was romantic passion and strength, and black represented a duality of values – all that was prudent and humble, and, in contrast, that which was wicked and related to death (Pastoreau, 2010, pp.96-97).

The symbolic use of colour could be applied both to names and appearances. For example, the armour of the knight Blandín de Cornualla is described as red at the beginning of the story (Pacheco, 1983, p.29), probably showing his power and the predisposition to love he has not yet found.

The maidens of the fourteenth-century chivalry novels are mostly described in white garments. In this sense, many times, its appearance is preceded by the arrival of a magical animal, also described as white. Before arriving at the enchanted castle where Brianda sleeps under the spell, Blandín finds a mysterious lady in the forest riding on a white stallion. The maiden, who serves enchanted food in order to make him fall into a deep sleep, changes the knight's horse for the white one which will lead him to Brianda's haunted castle (Pacheco, 1983, p.49).

In the text *Salut d'amor*[10], there can be found another example in this regard. This literary piece is a love epistle in

10. Technically, the term *Salut d'amor* defines a medieval literary typology, a lyric-narrative genre of Occitan or French origin, commonly written in paired verses. Generally its structure heads a greeting to the lady, the subsequent praise of her physical and moral beauty, and finally a loving confession with a request for returned feelings; all of this sometimes accompanied by arguments in favour of the lover with the use of illustrations, examples of court casuistry and even allegorical and sentimental short stories. In Catalonia, there were the two greetings of the troubadour Amanieu de Sescars (1278-1290), the anonymous works entitled *Letra amorosa* (1395), *Ruegos de amor, Requerimiento que hizo un fraile a una monja*, the hybrid *Stores del amado Frondino y de Brison*, elaborated at the beginning of the 15th century, and the important *Salud de amor* o *Clamor de amor*, elaborated at the end of the 14th century. It is only this last that will be referenced throughout this study.

verse in which the author tries to convince and seduce a married woman through the use of two interesting stories, the second a fantasy creation. This story seems particularly interesting because it tells how a noble lady and her lover knight arrive at a miraculous fountain where seven ladies who have yielded to romance appear. They are followed by seven cursed ladies who are expelled from the source of water by the Love god. These extraordinary acts convince the lady that she must give her love and charms to the knight before life withers.

In the story of *Salut d'Amor*, the knights find a great white deer during the hunting day, and then the main character and his lord's wife arrive at the magic fountain. The seven ladies who appear to convince her ride on white horses (Badia, 2003, p.106). The symbology of the number in this account shows how a completely fantastic story can have allegorical intentions. Seven is the number of everything complete in the Christian imagery: God created the world in seven days, seven are the days of the week and seven are also the joys of the Virgin Mary. For example, in *Tirant lo Blanch*, seven maidens make a representation of these joys (Martorell, 1490, vol I, p.92).

The ladies of *Salut d'Amor* show by their number the perfection and fullness of love. It is remarkable how the author describes them not only on the backs of white horses but dressed in golden robes.

Is there any reason for the author of this story to describe them like this? First of all, it should be noted that the writer of *Salut d'Amor* intended to get the affection of a married lady, arguing that she must give in to committing a minor sin to prevent a major crime: leaving her lover to die from the despair of not having his feeling retuned. To a point, his request cannot be described as chaste in the social context of the moment, so he cannot dress the ladies of his story with the chaste white of the maidens. He describes them instead with what seems to be established as the colour of the god of love: gold. After the appearance of the seven blissful ladies in the clearing of the fountain, a young knight dressed in full gold armour arises (Badia, 2003, p.108) and ends up being identified as the god of love.

There are many mentions of garments and ornaments made of gold in these novels—so many that it is impossible to ignore them. In the novel *Frare-de-goig i Sor-de-plaser*, the sleeping princess is completely covered with a golden cloak and, when the prince uncovers her, the girl wears a white shirt with embroidery, as was common at the time (Borrau , 1992, p.7) yet made of gold (Badia, 2003, p.120). Tirant lo Blanch and his love Carmesina are buried at the end of the novel dressed in gold garments. The same novel reasons that this occurs because the golden garments never wither or spoil (Martorell, 1490, vol II, p.408).

Based on this mention, we fully understand why the material is related to the God of love in allegories and all that it entails: gold is the most noble and precious material and, like true love, it is imperishable, ultimately eternal.

This colour seems to rival black in its use, the latter being widely used throughout the period. In literary texts, it is not often mentioned in a way that reflects its wide use in the reality of the time – used in penances, duels and much more (Marangues, 1991, p.113). It was established as an ambiguous symbol since, depending on its saturation, it could represent the best qualities or the worst. The intense black was a symbol of humility, modesty, temperance, authority and dignity. In contrast, matte and faded black was the eternal synonym of dirt, sin and death, the perfect symbol of hell and darkness. Also, and most importantly, it was always related to the symbolic denial of sexual life, which promoted its use among wise men, nuns and priests.

It is understood then that the ladies punished by the god Love are described as dressed in black and mounted on black horses in *Salut d'Amor* (Badia, 2003, p.107), as well as those knights in black armour[11] who must face Blandín and Guillot Ardit throughout the novel before obtaining his reward.

Despite everything, we see a change in the use of black in the development of chivalry novels: Güelfa, as a widow, wears it throughout the novel and is widely envied for it, which is explained by the historical reality contemporary to the elaboration of the novels of chivalry of the fifteenth century: the fashion of black exploded at that time as a result of the new advances in the Italian dye industry that finally achieved saturated and bright colours of these shades at a level the world had not seen before. Black also became in Catalan lands not only the representative colour of widows, but also the most desired. Any pretext was used to wear it, from the liturgies, that were considered sad, to the self-imposition of long mourning for distant relatives (Navarro, 1994, p.214). There can be found many descriptions of the beauty of those who are allowed to wear black, causing the envy of maidens sometimes.

As shown in *Curial e Güelfa*, it can be read as follows:

---

11. Armour is considered in this study as part of the clothing because of the behavior that was common in medieval courts. Medieval nobility generally used two types of armour, one which was rudimentary but prepared for battle, and a second the function of which was clearly of social representation. The latter was made with precious materials with gold inlays and valuable stones, and was combined with matching clothes, being given a reserved use for the time spent at court. In terms of its practical use, it was as any other garment made of fabric. For further information on this topic, it would be recommended that the investigations of Riquer (1968), the great historian of medieval Catalan armour, be consulted.

...e jatsia la Güelfa, com a viuda, fos de negre vestida, emperò
la sua gràcia era tanta que paria que la honestat d'aquelles
negres vestedures cresqués la sua bellesa. Laquesis la mirava
de fit en fit, e no partie d'ella la sua vista. Miraven-la tots los
cavallers e gentils hòmens...

(...Güelfa, as a widow, was dressed in black, but her grace
was so great that it seemed that the honesty of those black
robes increased her beauty. Laquesis looked at her from the
bottom to the end, and did not take her eyes off her. All the
knights and gentlemen looked at her...)

(Anon., 1435-1462, p.324)

It is really fascinating to see how the novels of the time
reflect the evolution of fashion and even reflect the change of
concepts, ideals, expectations and love relationships. They are
established as an open door to an era.

*

As a conclusion, and after analysing in detail the four basic
characteristics listed at the beginning of the study, it can be
firmly stated that the garments described in the Catalan chivalry
novels of the fourteenth and fifteenth century are more than just
a narrative amusement. They seem to establish themselves as
a symbology of the state of the characters in general, and their
love inclinations in particular.

Whether these kinds of symbology can be unravelled in
Arthurian medieval fantasy or other fantasy novels of the time
across all Europe remains a research project that is still to be
elaborated.

The descriptions of clothing and the attitudes that hide
loving messages in the Catalan chivalry novels, despite

being embedded in a world of wonderful fantasy, seem to be a reflection of the reality of the moment in the lands and kingdoms that produced these works. Some of these realities are not completely alien to readers nowadays – how many times have we seen a couple attend in matching attire at an event? Rings, gold and other materials and symbols continue to show eternal love beyond the pages of fantasy novels. The reality hidden in the landscape of fiction stories of the past and the present reflected – and will continue to reflect – who we were and who we are. This is a magical and romantic reality in itself, because it establishes the fantasy novels of the past as a mirror in which we can see ourselves reflected today, because the world changes and times pass, but human beings remain the same.

Bibliography

Anon., 1435-1462. *Curial e Güelfa*. Reprint 1979. Barcelona: Edicions 62 and La Caixa.

Badia, L., 2003. *Tres contes meravellosos del segle XIV*. Reprint with introduction of some anonymous Catalan novels. Barcelona: Cuaderns crema, Barcelona.

Badia, L. and Lamuela, X. ed., 1975. *Obra completa de Bernat Metge*. Barcelona: Selecta, Biblioteca Gasela.

Bonassie, P., Guichard, P. and Gerbet, MC., 2001. *Las Españas Medievales*, Barcelona: Crítica.

Borrau, C., 1992. *Cinc cents anys d'indumentària a Catalunya*. Barcelona: Labor.

Bernis, C.,1957. Indumentaria española del siglo XV: la camisa de mujer. *Archivo Español de Arte*, tomo 30, 119, p.187-209.

Dalmases, N., 1992. *Orfebreria catalana medieval: Barcelona 1300-1500: aproximació a l'estudi*. Barcelona: Institut d'Estudis Catalans, 2 vol.

D.I.E.C. Diccionari de l'Institut d'Estudis Catalans. Available at: <https://dlc.iec.cat/> [Accessed during 2018].

Lurie, A., 1994. *El lenguaje de la moda: una interpretación de la forma de vestir*. Barcelona: Paidós.

Macias, G. and Cornudella, R., 2011-2012. Bernat Martorell i la llegenda de Sant Jordi: del retaule als brodats. *Locus Amoenus*, 11, Universitat Autònoma de Barcelona, p.19-53.

Maranges I Prat. I., 1991. *La indumentària civil catalana. Segles XIII-XV*. Barcelona: Institut d'Estudis catalans.

Martínez Meléndez, Mª del C., 1989. *Los nombres de tejidos en castellano medieval*. Granada: Publicaciones de la Cátedra de Historia de la lengua Española.

Morgan, J., 2001. *Debrett's New Guide to Etiquette & Modern Manners*. New York: St. Martins press.

Martorell, J.,1490. *Tirant lo Blanch*, Reprint 1984. Barcelona: Edicions 62, (2 vol.).

Navarro Espinach, G., 1994. Los genoveses y el negocio de la seda en Valencia (1457-1512). *Anuario de estudios medievales*, 24, p.201-224.

Pacheco, A., 1983. *Blancdín de cornualla i altres narracions en vers dels segles XIV i XV*. Reprint with introduction of some anonymous Catalan novels. Barcelona: Edicions 62.

Pastoreau, M., 2010. *Azul: Historia de un colour*. Madrid: Paidós Ibérica.

Riquer, M.,1968. *L'arnés de cavaller: armadures catalanes medievals: Armes i armadures catalanes medievals*. Barcelona: Edicions Ariel.

Squicciarino, N., 1990. *El vestido habla*. Madrid: Cátedra, Signo e Imagen.

Yarza, J., 2003. *La nobleza ante el Rey: los grandes linajes castellanos y el arte en el siglo XV*. Madrid: Viso.

Contributors

Steph P. Bianchini is an Italian academic based in the UK. She's an Associate Professor and a member of the Royal Historical Society, and she has worked over the last ten years on projects in social sciences, international relations, and humanities.

She blogs about sciences, speculative fiction, and history at earthianhivemind.net and has had a book out in 2019 with Macmillan about the space sector.

As a fiction writer, Steph is a member of HWA and writes under the byline Russell Hemmell. Her short stories and poetry have appeared in 70+ publications, including *Aurealis*, *Flame Tree Press*, *The Grievous Angel*, and others.

Ezeiyoke Chukwunonso is a Ph.D. candidate at Manchester Metropolitan University. His research focuses on the impact of postcolonial theory on the evolution of Africa Speculative Fiction. A collection of his short story, *Haunted Grave and Other Stories* was published by Parallel Universe Publication.

Adam Dalton-West lectures in English and Creative Writing at Middlesex University. Under author name A J Dalton, Adam has published ten novels to date, including science fiction, fantasy and literary fiction. His main trilogy (*Empire of the Saviours*) with the publisher Gollancz Orion was listed for the Gemmell Award. He has also published best-selling titles such as *The Book of Angels* with Grimbold Books. In addition, Adam has published academically on science fiction, fantasy and horror. Indeed, his latest book - *The Satanic in Science Fiction and Fantasy* - is now available.

Tatiana Fajardo is a PhD candidate at the University of the Basque Country researching Patrick McGrath's Gothic fiction. She completed her MLitt in the Gothic Imagination at the University of Stirling (Scotland), writing her dissertation on the employment of art and science in Patrick McGrath's novels. She began a blog in which she discusses her literary, cinematic and artistic interests in 2017. Passionate about Gothic literature, her blog post on Dracula's "Bloofer Lady" was published by Sheffield University. Some of her essays have been translated into Swedish and published by Rickard Berghorn, both on his online *Weird Webzine* and in his printed books *Studier I vart* (2018) and *Två fantasistycken* (2018). These include her analyses of Ridley Scott's *Blade Runner* (1982) and Ingmar Bergman's *Hour of the Wolf* (1968). She presented her study of the employment of Romantic poets in the TV series *Penny Dreadful* (2014-2016) at the IGA conference in Manchester in August 2018. In 2019, her article "The Bloodlust of Elizabeth Báthory: From the Brothers Grimm to American Horror Story" was included in the book *A Shadow Within: Evil in Fantasy and Science Fiction* by Luna Press Publishing. Tatiana combines her work as a researcher with her job as an English teacher in Spain.

Christina Lake is a researcher, writer and science fiction fan based in Cornwall. She completed a PhD on eugenics in utopian fiction with Exeter University in 2017 whilst working as an academic librarian. Her SF short stories have been published in *Interzone* and various anthologies. She has also won awards for fan writing and was one of the guests at Follycon, the 2018 British Eastercon. She is now planning to pursue research interests in utopian fiction, SF, evolution, eugenics and genetics.

Cheryl Morgan is a writer, editor, publisher and critic. She owns Wizard's Tower Press and has written for a variety of outlets including *Locus*, *The SFWA Bulletin*, *SFX*, *Clarkesworld*, *Strange Horizons*, *Holdfast Magazine* and *SF Signal*. She is, to her knowledge, the first openly transgender person to have won a Hugo Award.

In addition to her science fiction interests she also co-hosts a women's interest show in Ujima Radio and lectures widely on transgender history.

Lynn O'Connacht is an aroacespec indie SFF author, freelance editor and independent researcher in asexuality and aromanticism studies. Lynn holds an MA in creative writing and English Literature. Lynn's fiction often centralises asexual and/or aromantic experiences within an SFF context and Lynn's research focuses on analysing the ways in which (SFF) literature uses asexual and aromantic tropes. It is Lynn's fervent hope that one day society will find a good way to tease apart the conflation of asexuality and aromanticism in earlier texts and settle on more nuanced language to discuss people's many and varied experiences.

Dr Ester Torredelforth, PhD in medieval art and illustrator, began her apprenticeship with the acclaimed painter Pere Ripoll i Calderó at the age of 7. At such early age, she showed a strong tendency towards medieval art, illustration and everything that surrounds it.

She developed her career at Rovira i Virgili University, where she ended her Doctoral studies in medieval fashion with a thesis titled "*Catalan Female Noble Clothing from the 15th Century and its Reflection in Art*".

Nowadays, she combines her artistic career with art teaching, and her activity in the medievalist research world, through several publications. Her latest works as illustrator are collaborations with acclaimed spanish poets like Enric Lopez Tuset and Adriana G. Garcia and collaborations with publishers in Madrid like Polibea Editorial and Hyperion Ediciones.

Barbara Stevenson is a fiction writer based in Orkney. She studied creative writing as part of a BA from the Open University. In 2016 she won the Scottish Association of Writers 'Castles in the Air' award for a fantasy short story. Her background in veterinary medicine has led to a growing interest in the portrayal of animals in fairy tales and folklore.

Cheryl Wollner's fiction and nonfiction appear in the anthologies *Today, Tomorrow, Always; Hashtag Queer Vol. 3*; and *The Best of Loose Change Anthology*. They are the winner of Pulp Literature's 2018 Raven Short Story contest for their story "Girls Who Dance in the Flames". Currently, they are pursuing their MFA in fiction at Florida Atlantic University where they are writing an alternate history novel about Bess and Harry Houdini.

Josephine Maria Yanasak-Leszczynski is the author of the post-Lovecraftian novel *A Coven in Essex County* (Visitant, 2016), and a contributing essayist to the film criticism work at Gayly Horror. Her criticism and words have appeared on *FemHype*, *FemPop*, and elsewhere. When not writing, she is presenting papers and moderating panels on the role of gender and sexuality in genre fiction.

Lightning Source UK Ltd.
Milton Keynes UK
UKHW021048140821
388796UK00007B/231